ALICE PAGÈS

WORLD VEGAN

GRUB STREET • LONDON

FOReWORD

Take your taste buds on a delectable journey! One thing is certain, you won't put down this book without experiencing a great burst of flavour and inspiration. Alice Pagès' cuisine is exactly like her photos: ultra-flavoursome, creative and inspired by cuisines from all over the world. From her culinary memories and extensive travels, she has gathered new ideas for combining different types of cuisines and cultures.

Based on healthy raw materials that are packed with nutrients and flavour, her approach to plant-based cooking is also unique. Reinventing many basic preparations and the ingredients used for them, some dishes are gluten-free, often made with little sugar and inspired by the techniques of vegan and raw cuisine. More than an invitation to travel, this book is an invitation to rethink how we cook. Alternatives to deep-frying, desserts brimming with flavour but with less sugar, pulses used in unexpected ways – these are all ideas that offer new variations to embrace in our daily lives. This book doesn't simply take traditional dishes from around the world and turn them into vegan versions. Rather, it's an innovative and very personal book, offering unique recipes with exciting flavour combinations and surprising, honest and astounding textures, like her recipe for hot dogs made with oyster mushrooms and topped with a satay sauce.

Inspired by traditional cuisines – in particular Asian, American and European street food – Alice offers you incredible sandwiches and dishes for sharing that are a true reflection of the convivial nature of food from around the world. Her personal culinary culture is also marked by French traditions, for both savoury and sweet recipes, yet always, of course, with her own personal twist and her own creative touch such as her churro-like French toast. Throughout all of Alice's recipes, you'll notice a constant dialogue between different culinary cultures. In the 1990s, her cooking would probably have been labelled 'fusion' because of the way she approached techniques and traditions to create something new, yet familiar, in the way that Californian cuisine was one of the wellsprings of modern vegan cooking.

More than a radical culinary change, Alice's dishes offer us a truly sensory experience. They draw on today's plant-based cuisine, on her personal history, on culinary traditions from all around the world and healthy cooking, and on every ingredient, enabling her to offer us ultra-creative recipes bursting with flavours.

And if, like me, you share Alice's love of peanut butter, you'll enjoy this book even more!

MARIE LAFORÊT

CONTENTS

Preface 6

Introduction

Eating better, for yourself and for the planet 10

Cooking, a world without borders 12

How to balance travelling and plant-based food 14

Getting away is just a stone's throw from home 16

Spices, the world at your fingertips 18

The larder 24

Basic equipment and utensils 30

Some tips before getting started... 32

BREAKFAST 34

Cinnamon rolls 36

Chocolate chip and coconut macatias 39

Danish pastries filled with cream and raspberries 40

Fluffy pancakes and miso caramel 43

Cocoa smoothie bowl and mini cereal cookies 44

Sweet potato smoothie bowl and tropical toasted granola 47

Crunchy nut and chocolate granola 48

Creamy porridge, roasted apples and caramel 50

French toast rolled like churros 53

Sweet potato toast, chocolate spread and homemade jam 54

Soft cookies with seeds and dried fruit 57

Savoury English breakfast porridge 58

Pretzel burgers, vegetable patties and scrambled chickpeas 61

Peanut hummus and shiitake mushrooms 62

SANDWICHES 64

Tomato pan-bagnat and crushed chickpeas 67

Baguette sandwich with marinated tofu, pesto and grilled pepper 68

The ultimate cheese burger 70

Naan stuffed with mashed pumpkin, hazelnuts and capers 73

Oyster mushroom hot dogs and satay sauce 77

Crunchy bánh mì burgers 78

Pita bread stuffed with red lentil falafel 80

Melted grilled cheese sandwich and roasted pear, rocket pesto and pickles 83

Burrito with creamy pumpkin and quinoa 84

BLT: the famous aubergine bacon, lettuce and tomato sandwich 87

MAINS 88

Socca, bean salad with fresh herbs and a lemony tahini dressing 90

Ratatouille chachouka-style with quinoa 93

Tomato and garden peach salad, fresh almond cheese 95

Baked aubergine with yoghurt sauce and dukkah 96

Mushroom and leek risotto with praline-coffee dressing 99

Silky mac and cheese with creamed vegetables 100

Spaghetti cacio e pepe with non-dairy parmesan 102

Caesar-style kale and crunchy chickpea granola salad 105

Breaded cauliflower, polenta fries and petit pois mayonnaise: my version of fish and chips 106

Creamy and crispy quiche Lorraine with filo pastry 110

Palak paneer: creamy spinach and chickpea curry 112

Rice pilaf with spices and dried fruit 115

Red lentil dahl, sautéed rice and cucumber salad 116

Yellow vegetable curry with pineapple and rice crackers 118

My version of Réunion's rougail sausage 121

Spring bowl with rice vermicelli, crispy vegetables and grilled tempeh 122

Mie goreng with tempeh and sautéed vegetables 124

Bakso: Indonesian dumpling and noodle broth 127

FOR SHARING 128

Provençal aïoli with al dente vegetables 130

Rocket and pistachio pesto mini-babkas 133

Herb crackers, hummus, tapenade and tomato caviar 134

Tortilla de patatas with creamy roasted peppers 137

Quick pissaladière for spur-of-the-moment appetisers 138

Nachos, broccoli guacamole, pico de gallo and cheese sauce 141

Rougail and vegetable achard as made in La Réunion 142

Réunionese chilli bonbons 144

Sweet potato, peanut and mango samosas 146

Empanadas stuffed with chilli and potatoes 148

Crispy cauliflower nuggets with chimichurri sauce 151

Alicia's tacos, shredded jackfruit and mole sauce 152

Korean kimchi pancakes with raspberry sauce 155

Baozi: steamed buns stuffed with mushrooms and kimchi 156

sweet snacks 158

Soft caramel, pretzel and hazelnut cookies 161

Lemon and black sesame muffins 162

The best peanut butter and chocolate chip banana bread 165

Provençal brioche Tarte de Saint-Tropez with verbena and strawberries 167

Raspberry, pistachio and white chocolate melt-in-the-mouth blondies 168

Doughnuts filled with homemade apple butter and caramel sauce 171

Custard tart with prunes and salted caramel 172

Soft chocolate, almond and orange blossom babka 174

Coconut dulce de Leche alfajores 176

Creamy chocolate hummus and crunchy biscuits for dipping 179

Carrot mug cake and cream cheese 181

Crunchy almond and aniseed biscuits 183

Apple, walnut and buckwheat crumble with tahini sauce 184

Fluffy crêpes with chocolate sauce 186

Desserts 188

Millionaire peanut and caramel shortbread 190

Rustic apricot tart with lemon and rosemary-almond cream 192

Lebanese rice custard pudding with orange blossom, rose and pistachios 194

Triple chocolate brownie mousse cake 196

Tropical coconut, mango, passion fruit and puffed rice bars 199

My childhood's chocolate-raspberry ice cream 200

Hazelnut pralines 202

Amazing banoffee cheesecake 204

Citrus trifle, coconut Chantilly cream and caramelised popcorn 207

Mont Blanc creams with caramelised buckwheat and hazelnut crunch 210

Coconut-mango milk sticky rice rolls and peanut sauce 213

Spiced, dried fruit sticky toffee puddings 215

Lightly spiced coffee tiramisù 216

Matcha and sesame mochi stuffed with red bean paste 218

Creamy rice pudding and coffee praline sauce 220

Index 222

Acknowledgements 224

PREFACE

More than a collection of recipes, this book invites you to travel. Filled with memories, encounters, discoveries, it's a walk along the streets of Buenos Aires, a trip to the colourful market of Saint-Paul, a picnic at sunset by the Mediterranean... It's also an immense joy to share a little of my universe with you.

Although I love cooking, I had no inkling I'd end up spending so much time in the kitchen. After studying aeronautical engineering, I worked for three years as a propulsion engineer. Although gastronomy was still a far-off idea, the desire to travel and make others travel was already in my mind. Whenever I had the chance, I'd grab my backpack and discover a new corner of the world, whose riches have never ceased to amaze me. No matter if it was a weekend in Europe or a more distant destination, the call to travel was always irresistible. And that's when this all-consuming passion for cooking appeared.

I've been vegetarian since I was a teenager, but my conscience was roused when I started working and could choose whatever I put on my plate, and this led me to stop eating animal products altogether. But at that time I didn't really know how to cook and veganism was a fringe trend. What restaurants offered was still very limited, and you often had to make do with a plate of tasteless side dishes in the office canteen. That was when I realised I'd have to do something about it! I endeavoured, I experimented, I failed (often), I learnt and I kept going. Little by little, and with no outside help, I practised in my kitchen. A year later, the desire to learn grabbed me: I quit my job to live my passion for plant-based cooking and photography to the full.

On my travels to the four corners of the Earth, I discovered the wealth of each country's culinary culture, tasted wonderfully colourful and flavoursome dishes and enjoyed enriching human experiences. More than just being a necessity, I became aware of the importance of cooking in every culture, however different, and the major role it plays in people's lives. Whether for our everyday nourishment or for celebrations, food is often a felicitous vehicle for sharing. Cooking for others means caring for others. That was also when I discovered traditional cuisine; a cuisine that is simple, honest and humane but incredibly tasty, comforting and steeped in history. And, surprisingly, a cuisine where plants are at the heart of the dishes.

While plant-based cooking may be perceived as a new trend, thanks to its recent surge in popularity, especially in Western countries, it is in fact rooted in many ancient culinary traditions. Ayurveda, a recognised and widely practised ancient system of medicine in India, advocates a predominantly vegetarian diet consisting of natural raw foods. Rice, cultivated for thousands of years, is the staple food and the core of every meal for almost half the world's population. Like cereals, bread is part of the daily life of many human beings, and no British or French person will deny that. If we put things into context, we mustn't forget that meat and animal products were once luxury foodstuffs. They are very expensive to produce, requiring time, energy and a lot of resources (plants to feed the animals, water, infrastructure, etc.) for a result that is not particularly profitable. Meat has long been consumed in moderation or, for the most modest populations, very occasionally.

That's the approach to food I grew up with. My mother – from La Réunion – taught me that a balanced dish should always revolve around a cereal and a grain. She would then add lots of vegetables and sometimes tofu, but animal protein was not necessarily included. On my travels, I

have seen similar habits in many countries. In Costa Rican cuisine, *casado* – an emblematic and traditional dish – consists of rice, beans, fried plantain and salad, with animal protein as optional. The same goes for most South American countries. It was only later, with the proliferation of intensive livestock farming, that eating habits changed and meat became more and more a part of people's diet ... until it became the main element.

Back in France, this observation began to perplex me. I'm in Paris, the world's top gastronomic city, and I have to struggle to get a decent vegan dish on the rare occasions when I dare to venture out to a restaurant. Society – and many cooks – viewed plant-based cooking as bland, boring and uninteresting. That was over six years ago but it's clear that things have changed! The increase in meat consumption and the search for competitiveness have forced manufacturers to drive prices down. This has been done at the expense of the quality of animal feed and the living conditions of these creatures, which, in turn, has consequences for consumer health. Faced with major environmental issues, the revelation of catastrophic farming practices and repeated health scandals, people are gradually becoming aware of the importance of food, and this is supported by new generations determined to change consumption patterns. Plant-based cooking is booming. Numerous actors, entrepreneurs, enthusiasts and famous chefs have helped give it a new lease of life and return it to its rightful place: at the centre of our tables.

Via the recipes I share on my blog, my aim is to make plant-based food accessible and appetising for everyone. I fully believe that beyond a simple necessity, our food is a major lever for ecological and environmental issues, enabling each of us to decide to act by changing our consumption habits. Forget the clichés, responsible eating does not have to be at the expense of flavour. In fact, it's quite the opposite because plant-based cooking is a chance to veer off the beaten track, to give free rein to your creativity, to discover ingredients and to reinvent your way of cooking. Plants are still a new world, a blank sheet of paper with no rules, meaning that the possibilities are endless. This book is the culmination of a mission: to pass on my love of good food and everything I've learnt over the last few years. Via these recipes, inspired by popular traditions from around the world, you'll rediscover everyday cooking with fresh ingredients and astounding flavours.

I hope these recipes will bring you much joy and memorable moments in the kitchen and around the table. Enjoy the discovery!

ALICE PAGÈS

EATING BETTER, FOR YOURSELF AND FOR THE PLANET

Why think twice when you can choose to eat well? Food has the property of being able to reinvent itself endlessly, to evolve alongside people and adapt to each of us. When it comes to choosing how we consume, we have a great responsibility to do so in a way that respects the planet and its inhabitants. Food is a major lever in the fight against climate change as well as in our transition, and most of us have the chance to act on that. The way we eat influences farming and livestock practices, which have a direct impact on the environment and society.

HOW TO BE A RESPONSIBLE CONSUMER EVERY DAY

RETHINKING WHAT'S ON YOUR PLATE

Industrial meat production has a devastating impact on the environment. It leads to deforestation just to grow animal feed, to water pollution, to greenhouse gas emissions, not to mention the matter of animal welfare and the negative impact on our health. These are all reasons to reduce meat consumption. It couldn't be easier to do as the world has a wealth of plants. It's estimated that there are over 400,000 plant species in the world, of which about 20% are edible. There are 80,000 varieties of fruit, vegetables, cereals, mushrooms, seaweed and flowers available for us to eat and enjoy. It's about rethinking the way we cook. Pulses, seeds and cereals contain enough protein to meet our daily needs. So rather than systematically trying to replace meat, let's try to compose a delicious and colourful dish.

COOKING WITH RAW INGREDIENTS

Healthy responsible eating means taking a good look at foodstuffs. Ready-made meals and processed foods have distanced us from our kitchens and the Earth. If you want to change the way you eat, my first piece of advice is to work as much as possible with raw produce, fruits, vegetables, grains and pulses. This allows us to reconnect with the food we eat on a daily basis and offers us the best taste and nutritional qualities while also avoiding packaging. Thanks to the recipes in this book you'll see that it's a breeze, and I can assure you that you'll get the hang of it in no time!

EAT LOCAL AND SEASONAL FOOD AS MUCH AS POSSIBLE

There are over 400,000 edible plants in the world, yet fewer than 20 species now provide 90% of our food, so try to broaden your choices. Seasonal fruit and vegetables, harvested when ripe – when they contain the most nutrients – are incomparable when it comes to quality of taste. Nature is ingenious, and the plants she offers us follow one another through the cycle of the seasons to give us exactly what our bodies need throughout the year. Eating locally and seasonally also allows you to discover forgotten ingredients, revealing a variety of flavours and reducing your environmental impact as fewer pesticides are needed for their cultivation. In addition, it's important to limit transport-related pollution, promote your local area and support the local economy, all the while lowering the cost of your shopping basket.

FIND OUT MORE AND MEET THE PRODUCERS

Behind every product you see on the shelves and every forkful you put in your mouth, there are men and women, know-how and history. Food labels (fair trade, organic farming, etc.) are already a good indicator of how foodstuffs are grown and what producers are paid. They certify compliance with specific economic, social and environmental standards. However, labels alone are not necessarily a guarantee of quality. It's important to find out about the produce and products you're buying, stay informed, talk to the sellers and producers when you go to the market, and even, if you have the chance, go and visit them on their farms.

COOKING, A WORLD WITHOUT BORDERS

"Cooking is the art of instantly transforming history-filled foodstuffs into joy."

Guy Savoy

"The most important ingredient to cook with is culture."

Massimo Bottura

There are so many ways to discover a culture! By travelling, of course, but also through music, art, sport, architecture, nature and, above all, food. Culinary culture — an ensemble of dishes, foodstuffs, rituals and ways of eating — has always galvanised society in every civilisation. It's what defines our way of life, gives our daily life rhythm, dictates our habits, brings us together, gives us a strong identity and the feeling of belonging to a group, to a family. It's also what connects us to the land, to our terroir, and to all those wonderful foodstuffs that are our most valued heritage and of which we are so proud.

TRAVELLING TO GET CLOSER

Of course, culinary culture differentiates us, but above all it brings us together regardless of whether it's within a community, a family sharing a good meal, or even between different cultures through the sharing of know-how and wealth of resources. How many wonderful encounters, how many incredible dishes, revolutionary inventions, historic decisions and unforgettable moments have been made possible by the confluence of two gastronomies? Taking the time to discover a cuisine means opening your mind to others, understanding a culture in its natural form and being on intimate terms with it. Because I'm curious and eager to discover new things, travel has always been important in my life. As a child, I spent a summer in the Galapagos Islands observing the endemic fauna; I went to London alone to learn English; and to Réunion Island to celebrate end-of-year holidays with my family. It is these experiences and moments that have shaped my career and my cooking.

TRADITIONAL CUISINE: THE NEW GASTRONOMY

This book will take you to the four corners of the world and (I hope) to discover flavours, foods and techniques borrowed from the world's traditional cuisines. Traditional cuisine literally means a way of cooking and preparing food that belongs to people; in other words, everybody's cuisine. A cuisine that is honest and affordable with uncomplicated techniques, it is also festive and full of flavour. I also see it as a cuisine that is generous and made for sharing.

Traditional cuisine is a sign of identity and it tells the story of a country. In many countries, for example, each region has its own age-old specialities, generally rooted in traditional cuisine: sauerkraut in Alsace, ratatouille in Provence, galettes in Brittany and raclette in Savoie, to name just a few. And in the UK, there is laverbread in South Wales, haggis in Scotland, pork pies in Melton Mowbray and Cornish pasties in Cornwall, among others. Influences from other countries, brought in by immigrants over centuries, have enhanced these traditional dishes. That's how such well-known and popular dishes such as couscous and tiramisu have enriched our culinary culture. Traditional cuisine is therefore a result of this melding and is constantly evolving. Today, many long-forgotten dishes are back in the spotlight, setting a trend and, in turn, reshaping the culinary landscape. Fed up with industrial foodstuffs that all taste the same, these new generations of cooks are seeking to return to a true and authentic cuisine. This is what I have tried to convey through the multi-cultural recipes in this book. It's not a question of offering you yet another hamburger, but of revisiting it in my own way by, for example, combining it with Vietnamese *bánh mì* to create a new dish.

HOW TO BALANCE TRAVELLING AND PLANT-BASED FOOD

As I point out in the opening pages of this book, plants are at the core of traditional cuisine in many countries. While it's fairly easy to eat vegetarian food when travelling, it's much more complicated when you also want to avoid dairy, eggs and any other animal foodstuffs. Some destinations require less effort than others: it's easier to eat vegan in Costa Rica, or in a big city where there's a wider range of foods, than in a remote part of Argentina where *asado* (traditional barbecue) is a veritable institution. To overcome these difficulties and get the best experience from your trip, here are some tips to help you eat vegan and local during your stay.

GOING TO FARMERS' MARKETS

Nothing is more fascinating than wandering through the stalls at a traditional market. And it's the best way to immerse yourself in the culture of a country. The smells and atmosphere create an authentic experience, and it's a great opportunity for making a picnic using local produce. The advantage of a market is that you're sure to find fresh, tasty, unprocessed foods and you know exactly what you're eating. Seasonal vegetables, homemade bread, fruit for dessert, and there you have it, plenty to enjoy on the go or for breakfast the next day.

TAKE PART IN A COOKING CLASS OR ENJOY A MEAL AT A LOCAL'S HOME

The best way to be sure of what you have on your plate is to do it yourself. And who better than the locals to show you their true traditional cuisine? As well as being an incredible human experience, taking part in a traditional cooking class or having a meal at the home of a local gives you a glimpse of another side of a country's culture. Obviously, you'll need to let the organiser or your host know of any dietary requirements beforehand. But believe me, the desire to share and to please is often so great that they'll be happy to adapt. It's also a great opportunity to discuss your choices and learn more from each other.

VISIT FARMS AND ARTISANS' WORKSHOPS

Many farms and small businesses welcome visitors, that is, if they're not already a tourist activity. In Sri Lanka, tea plantations are a staple on tourist tours, while in Italy you can visit beautiful citrus groves. And visiting a market is a great opportunity to talk to producers and take home the best of what is produced locally.

PREPARING YOUR TRIP

With all the tools available today, the growing interest in gastronomy and the feedback from many travellers, it's never been easier to organise a trip from home. Find out about local specialities, write down some vocabulary, look out for traditional markets and make a list of restaurants that offer plant-based food or that can adapt dishes. The internet is full of blog posts and there are many apps to make the task easier.

KEEP AN OPEN MIND AND BE FLEXIBLE

A final, and perhaps most important, piece of advice is to be open-minded and understanding. Not everyone you meet will be aware of what veganism is nor what it means to you. Vegetarianism is a personal choice and may not be compatible with some cultures or standards of living. Take the time to explain and discuss the reasons behind your choices. Sometimes you'll have to be flexible and bend your habits, perhaps getting away from the typical 'starter-main course-dessert' meal or eating 'only' two meals a day. Casting aside your daily routine to experience another way of life is also another reason for travelling.

GETTING AWAY IS JUST A STONE'S THROW FROM HOME

For a long time, I swore by far-flung travel and exotic destinations. I felt that I had to travel many kilometres to truly experience a change of scenery. In fact, this quest for 'even further, even more unusual' meant I was missing out on countless riches. A journey doesn't only start at the airport terminal. Escaping can be as simple as opening a cookbook to prepare a nice dinner or going to a local restaurant. Cooking has an exceptional ability to transport our senses and create emotions through the flavours and memories it evokes. As for ingredients, via their taste, fragrance and texture, they embody a cultural identity, a terroir, a history and are already part of the journey.

The simplest and most direct way to travel is through food in restaurants. In Britain, as in many countries, we are lucky to have a rich, varied and dynamic culinary scene. It's common for the same city or neighbourhood to have several traditional Indian, Asian, Lebanese, Mexican, African and other eateries. There's something for every taste and every budget. These places allow you to discover cuisines that are completely traditional, or revisited according to the whim of the chef.

Markets are also good places for travelling. You can often find stalls specialising in one type of world cuisine, particularly street food. It's not uncommon to enjoy tacos, empanadas or samosas in the market itself or buy a curry and fried rice to take away.

But if you like cooking, the best way to get away is to get into the kitchen! There's nothing more stimulating than following a recipe step-by-step and discovering a new dish, or simply following your own desires with the ingredients at hand to make a delicious homemade dish. Here are some recommendations to bring a daily and exotic touch to your dishes.

A LOOK AT SPICES

I'll come back to this further on in more detail, but spices are a great way to add a novel touch to your cooking and to reinvent your day-to-day dishes. So, the taste of a vegetable curry will be different depending on the spices you use.

BE BOLD AND USE CONDIMENTS

Condiments and in particular fermented foodstuffs, such as miso, soy sauce, vinegar, preserved lemon or black garlic, are great for adding character to a dish. Because they tend to have a pronounced taste, you only need to use a little to intensify flavours immediately. Although often found in specialised grocery shops (Asian, Indian, African, etc.), they're being produced locally more and more!

REINVENTING AND APPROPRIATING RECIPES

As you can see, this book aims to give you the basics, the inspiration and the confidence to get started and create your own unique recipes. With a little experience and practice, you'll realise that one vegetable can easily be swapped for another in your favourite recipe, meaning you can follow the seasons while bringing something new to your dishes.

SPICES, THE WORLD AT YOUR FINGERTIPS

Spices are an integral part of my cooking and I use them every day in my dishes. Whether used to flavour a curry or a vinaigrette, spices are a wonderful way to add character and depth to a dish, but also to enhance flavours. Spices also offer many health benefits, playing a major role in traditional medicines such as Ayurveda. They can be obtained from various parts of a plant: flower, fruit, seed, bark or root.

Most of the spices we know and use in the kitchen come from afar and are therefore imported and expensive. It's important to check the origin of the spices you buy and to use them sparingly. In the end, it's cheaper to buy good quality spices, which may be a little more expensive but whose flavours are more intense, so you can use less.

There are over a hundred spices in the world, all with their own specificities, unique flavours and uses in cooking. Here's a list of essential spices that are called for in this book's recipes.

INDIVIDUAL SPICES

Aniseed: aniseed has a very characteristic fragrance and a fresh sweet flavour. It can be used as a condiment for savoury dishes (salads and vegetables) as well as in desserts. It's commonly used in pastry making and confectionery. Aniseed is good for digestion: as an infusion it's just the thing after a heavy meal.

Cinnamon: without a doubt it's my favourite spice. Cinnamon is the bark from the young shoots of the cinnamon tree. Characterised by warm, rounded, woody sweet flavours that are both mild and intense, it's the spice of choice for desserts and pastries, such as the famous cinnamon roll.

Cardamom: another of my favourite spices. Cardamom is characterised by its great fresh and lemony, slightly peppery yet not pungent taste. Its very strong taste can quickly mask other fragrances, so it's best to use it sparingly. It goes well with many savoury dishes – and used in many curries – but I prefer it infused in coffee, Turkish style.

Coriander: a true symbol of Asian and Far Eastern cuisine, coriander seeds are characterised by a fresh, slightly peppery fragrance similar to citrus peel. Used in many stews such as couscous or tagines, it's also an ingredient in sweet recipes such as gingerbread, and even in condiments such as pickles.

Cumin: another essential spice in Indian curries and blends, cumin has a strong, peppery, slightly pungent flavour. It's a comforting spice that can beautifully enhance a simple butternut squash and carrot purée, or oven-roasted sweet potatoes.

Turmeric: dried and ground, this golden powder, with its sweet fragrance and warm, slightly musky flavour, is used in most curries to give them their characteristic colour. Turmeric has long been used as a substitute for the much more expensive saffron. In Réunion, it is called 'Bourbon saffron'. Turmeric is also a powerful antioxidant that helps keep your liver healthy.

Ginger: fresh ginger is characterised by a slightly lemony, intense freshness and a juicy texture. Dried ginger has warmer, peppery notes and a pungent flavour that awakens the taste buds. I love using it in desserts, drinks and breakfast dishes to add intensity, especially when combined with cinnamon and cocoa. Ginger is also a powerful antiseptic and anti-inflammatory.

Cloves: cloves have an intense, pungent flavour. Used in small quantities with other spices for both cooking and baking, they add depth. Cloves have been used for centuries to preserve food because of their antibacterial properties.

Nutmeg: with its warm, rounded and slightly sweet taste, nutmeg is best known for adding flavour and a certain oomph to milk and potato-based dishes, such as mashed potatoes and gratins. It also lends itself well to sweet dishes, particularly when combined with vanilla for roasted fruit in syrup, for example.

Paprika: ground paprika comes from the dried and ground fruit of the pepper (also known as sweet pepper). Unlike chilli, paprika has a sweet, rounded, fruity taste that gives vegetables an elegant flavour. I use it very often. As for smoked paprika, it has a spicy barbecue-like flavour. It's fantastic in marinades as it brings a smoky flavour, especially as it holds up well when cooked.

Pepper: probably the most common spice found in our kitchens. Black pepper is well known, but there are many varieties and origins, all of which differ in flavour and therefore in use. Pepper can be powerful and pungent, but also delicate, fresh, with cocoa, woody, vanilla and even smoky aromas. It's an essential spice for enhancing all types of dishes, both savoury and sweet.

Sumac: ground sumac comes from the berries of the eponymous shrub, which are dried and ground. Sumac is characterised by its tangy, fruity flavour and lemony notes. In combination with other spices, such as za'atar, it's used to season grilled vegetables, salads and hummus.

Tonka: a large, black seed that is grated. Tonka beans are a sweet, comforting spice with nutty, caramel-like aromas similar to vanilla. Moreover, tonka beans are a good alternative to vanilla for flavouring desserts.

Vanilla: sweet, sometimes floral or chocolatey, but always incredibly elegant, vanilla is unquestionably the queen when it comes to fragrant spices. It's easy to use in desserts, creams, custards, compotes and fruit salads, or to flavour hot drinks.

SPICE BLENDS

Although interesting individually, spices are even more incredible when combined. And it's not just about mixing flavours. Marrying spices is an art that requires sensitivity, mastery and knowledge. Some spices act in synergy and increase their properties and flavours tenfold. For example, in 'golden milk', an ancient Ayurvedic drink, turmeric is combined with pepper to help the body absorb it and ginger to boost its antioxidant action. Blends are also easier to use and are therefore ideal for learning about spices. Buy them ready-made or create your own recipes!

Chai: intense, warm and stimulating, chai is an absolute concentration of flavours. It can be used in cooking as well as in desserts or as a drink in the classic *chai latte*. I love adding it to winter cakes – think carrot cake – and it goes perfectly with nuts and dried fruit, bringing with it comforting flavours. It can also be infused in a syrup that's delicious with roasted fruit.

Chilli: piquant, lively, sweet and spicy at the same time, chilli blends consist of garlic, cumin, paprika and a small chilli from which it takes its name. It's the mainstay of chilli con carne, an icon of Tex-Mex cuisine, but it goes very well with all sunny dishes, in particular ones with a sauce. More surprisingly, the spicy flavour of chilli goes brilliantly with dark chocolate! Keep this in mind the next time you make hot chocolate.

Five-spice: a traditional blend from southern China, five-spice is one of the most widely used blends in the world. It's a subtle blend of five spices with citrusy notes, woody, warm and slightly sweet flavours. It's great for flavouring Asian dishes, stir-fried vegetables, stuffings, noodles, rice, as well as for marinating tofu or tempeh.

Curry: there are as many varieties of curry as there are people in the world who make it! This very popular Indian blend is found in all cultures under different names. The ingredients can vary, but usually turmeric, cumin, coriander and pepper dominate. Fresh, pungent and warm, it's used to make curries but also features in many other Indian dishes (dahl, rice, etc.) or simply to season a vinaigrette.

Dukkah: a pinch of this delicious crunchy blend of spices, seeds and roasted nuts sprinkled over a dish is enough to make it truly special. Originally from Egypt, dukkah is used as a finishing touch to summer salads, chilled soups, tabbouleh, grilled vegetables and hummus. It can be made in several ways, with or without the addition of roasted nuts, almonds or pistachios.

Gomasio: a Japanese mixture of sesame seeds and salt, traditionally used to season rice. Seaweed can also be added for a briny touch. It's an ideal condiment to place in the middle of the table and sprinkle on at the last moment on your salads, soups, vegetables, toast and rice.

Garam masala: this literally means 'hot spice mixture'. This traditional North Indian seasoning is characterised by its very rounded, warm spiciness yet is not piquant. It's used in Ayurvedic medicine to warm the body and soul. Like curry, it's used in many stews and rice dishes, but it can also be used as a substitute for traditional spices in desserts and cakes.

Herbes de Provence: a fragrant and powerful blend of Mediterranean herbs that concentrates the flavours of the Mediterranean's shrubby *garrigue* vegetation and of summer. Easy to use, these herbs can be sprinkled on grilled and roasted vegetables and are all you need to season ratatouille, pulses or a tomato tart.

Ras el-hanout: festive and captivating, ras el-hanout is a traditional Maghrebi blend that is perfect for couscous, tajines, chachoukas, rice and pasta. The ingredients can vary considerably: it can be made with 20 to over 30 different spices! It's characterised by warm flavours and a tangy floral fragrance.

Za'atar: warm, fragrant and intense, za'atar is the Middle East's flagship blend. Originally made with a variety of wild oregano, this can be replaced with dried thyme, roasted sesame seeds to add a delicious taste, roasted hazelnuts and sumac for a hint of acidity. Like gomasio and dukkah, za'atar can be sprinkled directly over prepared dishes and over salads, grilled vegetables and other summer dishes. A simple piece of soft bread dipped in olive oil and sprinkled with za'atar is something marvellous.

SPICES AND COOKING

Spices are fragile ingredients, the taste and nutritional qualities of which can change when cooked. This means they must be added just at the right time. For a stew or soup, it's best to add the spices after frying the onion and garlic. For a curry, it's best to fry them first in a little fat to intensify their flavour. In both cases, it's important to keep an eye on them to prevent burning. They can also be used in marinades and desserts.

I recommend toasting your spices whole for a few minutes in a dry frying pan to intensify their flavours. Cumin and coriander seeds benefit particularly well from this.

WHOLE OR GROUND?

Although ground spices are easier to use, there's much to be gained by using whole spices. Once ground, they get musty and quickly lose much of their fragrance. As these are rare and expensive products, it's best to have a range of whole spices that you can grind according to the amount needed and right before using them. You'll get optimal freshness and waste less.

For seeds, you'll need a mortar and pestle or a spice grinder. Other, harder seeds, such as nutmeg or tonka beans, need to be grated finely with a Microplane.

STORING SPICES

Spices are sensitive to light and damp or humid environments. To make sure they remain at their best, store them in clean, dry airtight glass bottles in a dark cupboard or drawer. If you buy spices in bags, transfer them to glass jars. When stored properly, some will keep for a year or more.

HERBS

The difference between a spice and a herb is a subtle one. Both are plants, but herbs alter the aroma of a dish thanks to their own fragrance, while spices enhance the taste. Herbs have more of an influence on smell as they perfume a dish, while spices influence the flavours by intensifying them.

Herbs are plants whose leaves are used fresh or dried. I prefer to use basil, coriander, chives, thyme, rosemary, mint, dill, parsley, tarragon, etc. fresh to preserve all their flavours and benefits. A few chopped basil or mint leaves are enough to elevate a salad, tabbouleh or roasted aubergines. The vast majority of herbs are easy to grow in a vegetable garden or indoors, which is very convenient as you can have fresh herbs on hand all year round!

Onions, shallots and garlic are also aromatic plants, but it's the stem or bulb that's eaten. Easy to cook, they are a great addition to many dishes. Depending on how they are prepared, their flavour can vary significantly: raw garlic is sharp and pungent, whereas it becomes very mild when cooked slowly. Garlic is one of my favourite ingredients, and I use it whenever possible. However, its strong taste is not for everyone, so feel free to adjust the quantities according to your liking.

AND FINALLY...

Other ingredients are more difficult to classify, but I think they deserve to be mentioned here, as they help to season and flavour dishes.

Salt is a unique ingredient that comes from the sea. Pink Himalayan salt, which has become increasingly popular, is a rock salt produced by the evaporation of the seas hundreds of millions of years ago. Himalayan black salt, or *kala namak*, is very sulphurous and its flavour is surprisingly like hard-boiled eggs. I use it in several of the recipes in this book to season omelettes and flatbreads. Salt can be refined, processed or flavoured, and comes in powder or crystal form. I prefer using fine salt in dishes where it's mixed in, and use delicate, fragrant and subtle fleur de sel for sprinkling over food. A touch of fleur de sel on cookies just out of the oven is enough to increase their flavour tenfold.

Cacao, obtained from fermented cocoa bean kernels, is different from chocolate. Cacao is unsweetened and has an intense, slightly bitter and tangy flavour. Cocoa powder or cocoa nibs can be used for both savoury (think of a wonderful Mexican mole sauce) and sweet dishes. To enjoy all its benefits and discover new flavours, try raw, unroasted cacao.

Orange blossom flavouring is obtained by distilling bitter orange flowers. It has a sweet, floral flavour and a characteristically sweet fragrance. It's used mainly to flavour pastries such as *navettes de Marseille*, brioches, creams and drinks.

Malted yeast, also known as 'nutritional yeast', consists of adding malted barley to brewer's yeast (a microscopic fungus obtained by fermenting malted barley) to achieve a milder taste. In addition to being high in vitamin B, it has a strong cheese-like flavour, which is why I use it very often in dishes that call for non-dairy cheese. It's usually found in flakes that can be sprinkled directly over salads and pasta.

THE LARDER

Plant-based cooking is often perceived as complicated because it sometimes calls for ingredients you may not be familiar with. However, it's a natural, authentic and economical cuisine that uses mainly raw ingredients. You may have to spend some money when you start out cooking vegan food, but it'll quickly pay for itself and you'll enjoy fresh, tasty and very nutritious food. I've included a list of the main ingredients you'll need to make most of the recipes in this book. Don't forget to read the notes at the bottom of each recipe for more detailed explanations.

CEREALS

Since the dawn of time, cereals have been a staple for most of the world's inhabitants. Rice, wheat, maize, oats and quinoa are well known, but there are many other equally interesting kinds such as rye, einkorn, buckwheat and millet. The advantage of the latter is that many of them are grown in Britain and Europe and tend not to be genetically modified. The vast majority of these cereals are easily found in supermarkets or organic grocery shops, which increasingly offer local and artisanal products. Also, consider buying in bulk to save money (they keep for a long time) or, just the opposite, buy only when you need to and so avoid waste.

PULSES

High in protein, nutritious and inexpensive, pulses are widely used in plant-based cooking; but not only that, they are also a staple food in cultures around the world. There are many varieties, the best known being peas, beans and lentils, and these are the ones I mainly use in my recipes. You can buy pulses dry or already cooked and in brine. Jarred food is very convenient and preserves practically all of the nutrients. This is the sort I recommend for most recipes. However, using dried pulses is best for certain dishes such as falafel or chilli bonbons from Réunion. Dried pulses have a different texture and flavour, and need to be soaked in water overnight before being cooked or used raw. As with cereals, a number of pulses are grown in Britain and sold in many shops: remember, buying in bulk can be cost saving.

SOYBEANS

Like beans, soybeans are a pulse and are used as a base for many foodstuffs such as tofu and tempeh. If possible, choose products that are made with British soybeans and are not genetically modified.

Eaten for centuries in Asia, tofu is made by coagulating soy milk and has become very popular in Britain in recent years. The curds, which are white and have a neutral taste, come in soft and firm form, so it's important to add flavour. Given its high protein content and an interesting consistency, tofu is very popular in plant-based cooking. Although there are many varieties, we'll look mainly at firm and silken tofu here. Firm tofu can be diced, marinated and fried, or crumbled. Silken tofu has a much smoother and creamier texture. When blended, it can be used to make sauces, smooth creams and batters. I use it, for example, to make *Far Breton* and quiche Lorraine.

Tempeh, which is less well known but just as interesting, originates from Indonesia and is made from fermented whole soybeans. It has a firmer texture than tofu and, because of the fermentation process it undergoes, a stronger flavour. My favourite way to eat it is sliced, marinated in tamari, sesame oil and a drizzle of maple syrup, then pan fried.

FLOURS AND YEAST

Flour is obtained by grinding and milling cereals such as wheat, or pulses such as chickpeas, and there are many varieties. For the recipes in this book, and for my daily cooking, I prefer flours that are easy to find, inexpensive, organic and produced locally. Sometimes, I also use gluten-free alternatives as they offer many possibilities and open up new outlooks. In addition to wheat flour, you'll need rice flour, maize flour, buckwheat flour and oat flour, which you can make yourself simply by blitzing rolled oats!

Cornflour, as opposed to maize flour, is a very fine powder – high in starch – used to bind and thicken sauces. It's great in pastry making for making lighter doughs, particularly for gluten-free recipes, thanks to its ability to bind.

You'll also need different types of yeast.

Baking powder – mainly used when baking cakes – creates a chemical reaction that gives off gas and makes dough rise. Baker's yeast however, is made up of living cells, and works by fermentation that also produces gas. Used in baked goods, bread and yeast doughs, it's what gives that good taste to fermented bread. It comes in two forms:

dry (granulated) and fresh (cubed). When making bread dough, pastries and buns, I prefer using fresh yeast. Fresh yeast is a living organism with a specific shelf life and should be kept somewhere cool and dry. It must be diluted and activated in a liquid at the right temperature, warm but not hot, ideally just below 37°C. You can swap it for dry yeast, but you'll need 2.5 times less.

OILSEEDS AND SEEDS

Nuts and seeds are vital ingredients in plant-based cooking. Not only are they excellent from a nutritional point of view, thanks to their unsaturated fatty acids (good lipids) and numerous micronutrients, but they also add texture and flavour to many dishes. Almonds, hazelnuts, cashews, walnuts, peanuts, sunflower seeds, pumpkin seeds, flaxseeds, sesame seeds, there's something for everyone! Oilseeds can be used as they are, whole or crushed, raw or toasted, to add crunch, for example to a salad. You can also find them in butter, powdered or drink form.

I use oilseed butters a lot in my sweet and savoury recipes, firstly for their irresistible taste, but also for their binding power, adding creaminess, stabilising flavours and replacing some of the fat. You can easily swap oilseed butters as their characteristics are very similar; it's mainly the taste that varies. So, you can swap peanut butter for almond butter in a cake, or with tahini if you're allergic to nuts.

I also use ground almonds and hazelnuts in many of my baked goods as a complement to flour as they add softness and lightness.

SOAKING

Some oilseeds benefit from soaking overnight as this removes the enzyme inhibitors that naturally surround and protect them. This makes them more digestible and releases the nutrients so that the body can absorb them more easily. This is particularly true of almonds, hazelnuts and walnuts. This step softens cashew nuts so that when you whiz them, you'll end up with very silky preparations.

TOASTING

Toasting oilseeds and seeds increases their flavour and crunchiness tenfold. Toast your own nuts and seeds instead of buying them already toasted, as they tend to be less nutritious and are often salty. To do this, brown them for about ten minutes in the oven at 180°C (gas mark 4). Whiz them in a powerful food processor to make your own butters. It's very satisfying.

WHAT ABOUT COCONUTS?

High in fatty acids, coconuts are an oleaginous fruit (similar to olives and avocados). I use coconut oil in many of my recipes, as well as coconut cream and flour.

PLANT-BASED 'DAIRY' PRODUCTS

Milks, creams, yoghurts and plant-based alternatives to dairy products have gradually taken up more space on supermarket shelves and are now very easy to find. The range of foodstuffs on offer continues to diversify, and there's now a wide choice of flavours and textures.

Milks and creams are mainly made from oilseeds (almonds, hazelnuts, cashews and coconut), cereals (oats, rice, buckwheat, spelt) or soy. Soy and almond products are the most neutral in taste, which makes them perfect for both savoury and sweet dishes. Cereal-based milks have a sweeter flavour and are therefore more suitable for desserts and milk drinks. Hazelnut and coconut milks, with their strong taste, are ideal for giving flavour. In general, and for the recipes in this book, choose organic, unflavoured milk with no added sugar.

When it comes to yoghurt, I mainly use soy and almond yoghurt. Coconut yoghurt is very rich and thick and is good in some desserts or for breakfast, with granola and fresh fruit. Greek-style non-dairy yoghurt, which has a thicker and smoother texture, is now slowly appearing on the market.

CONDIMENTS

Like spices, condiments are essential for seasoning dishes and adding flavour to meals. Sauces, pickles, chutneys, vinegars, etc. can be integrated into dishes, added at the end or served as an accompaniment. In addition to mustard and gherkins, there's a whole range of lesser-known flavours.

Miso is a fermented, salty paste from Japan. It can be made from soybeans, rice, barley or chickpeas, to which salt, water and a ferment called *koji* are added. In Japan, there are more than fifty types of miso. In Britain, brown, red and white miso are the most commonly available and can be found in Asian or organic grocery shops. The colour of a miso is a good indicator of its flavour: the darker it is, the stronger the taste. For the recipes in this book, you can use brown rice miso.

Pickles are vegetables that are marinated in a brine of vinegar and spices, and are characterised by a spicy, tangy and piquant taste. Gherkins are well known, but almost all vegetables and even fruit can be pickled! I've given several easy recipes in this book.

Lacto-fermented vegetables are made with fresh vegetables that are finely chopped and covered with a brine of water and salt, then left at room temperature for several days. The process of lacto-fermentation releases lactic acid, which preserves the vegetables and results in new and sometimes surprising flavours. Examples include kimchi – which I use in *baozi* and Korean pancakes – and vegetable achard, for which there's a recipe in this book.

Seaweed, not commonly used in Britain, is nevertheless an exceptional foodstuff. Very high in vitamins, minerals and trace elements, it's no wonder they've been an important ingredient in Asian cuisine for hundreds of years. Fresh, dried, whole or in flakes, seaweed affords the briny flavour of the sea to many dishes. Roscoff, in Brittany, is home to Europe's largest seaweed field, while off the coast of Scarborough, in North Yorkshire, is Britain's biggest seaweed farm. In

Roscoff, nori, kombu, dulse, wakame, sea lettuce and samphire are grown in an eco-friendly way. A true bonanza!

OILS

Vegetable oils – essential for cooking – fix flavours, bring texture, aromas and many nutrients to dishes.

For cooking and vinaigrettes, I prefer olive oil (a must in Mediterranean cuisine), as it's very fragrant and can withstand high temperatures. Sesame oil, with its toasted flavour, is ideal for marinades, sauces and pan-frying, and adds an exotic touch.

Grapeseed and sunflower oils, which are more neutral in taste, are perfect for baking.

For frying, sunflower oil and peanut oil are good alternatives.

Coconut oil is quite particular as it's liquid when heated and solid when cold. It's therefore great for making creams and uncooked desserts. It has a strong coconutty taste, so if you don't like it, buy the deodorised kind.

SWEETENERS

When it comes to sweetening food, there are many alternatives to refined white sugar. Natural unrefined sweeteners not only provide a subtle sweetening, but also interesting and varied flavours. I choose a sweetener depending on what I'm going to make.

Granulated sugars: pure cane sugar (such as muscovado or *rapadura*) and coconut sugar are unrefined sugars. As muscovado has quite a strong flavour you can't use the same amount as white sugar. Coconut sugar is sweeter, has a subtle caramelised taste and it is much lower on the glycemic index than white sugar.

Liquid sugars: maple syrup is my favourite! I use it by itself or combined with granulated sugar to add sweetness, moisture and flavour. It's also low on the glycemic index. Coconut flower, agave and yacon syrups are good tasty alternatives too.

Dried fruit: dried fruit (apricots, prunes, figs, grapes, cranberries, etc.) and in particular dates, which are naturally high in carbohydrates, add sweetness to many dishes, in addition to fibre and flavour. Medjool dates are juicy, sweet and have a lovely caramel taste. Once soaked and blitzed, they can be used to make delicious sauces.

Wherever possible, I try to use as little sugar as I can in my recipes, but you can taste and adjust the quantities to your liking.

10.3.21
citron sorente confit

BASIC EQUIPMENT AND UTENSILS

One of the advantages of home cooking is that it doesn't usually require expensive, high-tech equipment. With just a few basic utensils you can make all the recipes in this book. Here are the must-have accessories for you to enjoy cooking.

Good knives. Knives are a cook's main work tool. Essential for cutting, slicing, chopping, crushing and preparing ingredients properly, neatly and efficiently. A long-bladed chef's knife and a small paring knife are all you need for cooking comfortably and working with most ingredients, especially vegetables and herbs. Whether you're just starting out or want to improve your cooking skills, I strongly recommend investing in good knives. With careful use, good maintenance and regular sharpening, they will last for years, even a lifetime.

A potato peeler is used for peeling vegetables, but also for making beautiful ribbons. You can also use a Japanese mandoline, which is effective for slicing vegetables quickly and finely, but otherwise, a sharp knife will do.

Precision scales are indispensable in the kitchen and even more so for pastry making, where every gram is important. These allow you to weigh to the nearest gram, which is very useful for measuring light and active ingredients such as baking powder and agar-agar.

A thermometer with an electronic probe to accurately check the temperature of liquids and hot foods is also essential for frying, caramelising and tempering chocolate.

You'll also need a blender and/or food processor for crushing, grinding or whizzing ingredients. Personally, I use a blender/food processor with a large and a small bowl that I've had for years. A processor with an 'S' blade will also do the trick, and is ideal for dishes, such as hummus, where you want to keep some texture. If you want to make non-dairy milks, oilseed butters or ice creams using frozen fruit that require quite a bit of power, I suggest you invest in a good quality blender/food processor. For everyday preparations, you can use a stick blender, but it's less versatile.

An electric mixer is good for mixing large quantities of batter or for whipping cream. Most food processors and stick blenders come with this accessory.

A traditional oven with several cooking modes and several decks is enough for cooking and baking most foods efficiently and evenly. You'll also need suitable baking trays and parchment paper or a silicone mat.

Some pots and pans, preferably made of stainless steel and with heavy bottoms are best. Again, quality products are more expensive, but they'll last for many years.

A piping bag with a few tips is useful for decorating desserts and for piping fillings neatly. You can find reusable ones now. You can also use a freezer bag and cut off a corner.

Baking tins, muffin and pie tins, preferably made of sheet steel (which should be oiled well beforehand) or with a non-stick coating are best. Silicone moulds are practical but aren't great at conducting heat so not suitable for large items. Spring form pans are very practical for easily unmoulding cakes.

You'll need several different-sized bowls for mixing and storing what you've made.

And last but not least, you'll need spatulas of different materials, a whisk, and other small kitchen utensils.

SOME TIPS BEFORE GETTING STARTED...

Now that you have all your utensils at hand, it's time to begin! This book offers a variety of recipes: some are very simple, while others involve more steps. No matter if you're a beginner or a seasoned cook, there's something for everyone here and all the recipes are easy to follow. Here are my last and most valuable tips for cooking successfully.

Read through the entire recipe before you start. This will allow you to have an overall idea of the recipe and the different stages involved, and to organise yourself accordingly. Some recipes require a resting time, a rising time or part of the recipe to be made the day before.

Get your materials and ingredients ready before you begin. Good organisation and a clean and tidy worktop are a must in the kitchen. Having all the necessary utensils and ingredients at hand allows you to be efficient and focused.

Pay close attention to what you need to weigh. This goes for all recipes but even more for pastry making. Some preparations, such as doughs, batters and cakes, require ingredients to be weighed very precisely, especially when it comes to the correct amounts of active agents such as baking powder and agar-agar. When cooking, it's important to respect the weighing process as it ensures that amounts are correct and that the dish is balanced. If you change the number of servings in a recipe, remember to calculate and write down the amount of each ingredient before you start.

Regularly taste what you're making throughout the recipe, and feel free to adjust the seasoning according to the desired flavour but also to your taste. A dish is successful when it's balanced. Balance is built around the five flavours: acidic, bitter, sweet, salty and umami. We all have different perceptions of flavour, so feel free to add a touch of salt or acidity if you feel the need. If you've left out an ingredient, tasting as you go along will help you realise that.

Make sure that textures are correct. This is particularly important when making batters and doughs, whether a simple pancake batter, pie dough or leavened brioche dough. Even if you follow the measurements to the nearest gram and use the type of flour indicated in the recipe, you might not get the same result as me. For example, a T55 wheat flour from an artisanal mill will not be made from exactly the same kind of grain as a T55 from a mass-market brand, and so will give a different texture. It's therefore important to touch

and feel the dough, and if necessary to add just a little water or flour to get the right consistency. But first, make sure you've kneaded the dough long enough!

Also, respect and adapt the resting and baking times. A few minutes less or more baking time can make a big difference. This is especially true for pastry making and small items like cookies, but also for larger cakes that require a longer baking time to be fully cooked through.

It's essential always to respect the minimum baking time indicated, then check what you're making and adapt it if necessary. Some recipes, like leavened dough, need a resting time, and some desserts need to be chilled. Like baking times, these are very important to ensure that the active ingredients are totally activated, or that a mousse, for instance, sets properly. For leavened dough, resting times depend on the surrounding temperature.

BREAKFAST

CINNAMON ROLLS

The first time I ever tasted a cinnamon roll was in a small town in Norway, after a long cold day of hiking. That experience will forever be etched in my mind. First, it was the intoxicating aroma of cinnamon. Then there was the texture; soft and with a melt-in-the-mouth centre. And lastly, the inimitable taste of brioche and caramelised sugar.

MAKES 10 ROLLS
PREP TIME: 30 MINUTES
RESTING TIME: 2 HOURS 15 MINUTES
BAKING TIME: 18 MINUTES

FOR THE DOUGH
190 ml almond milk
6 g dried baker's yeast
4½ tbsp coconut oil
400 g T55 flour
30 g coconut sugar
1 tsp cardamom
5 g salt

FOR DECORATION
30 g coconut sugar
10 g cinnamon
50 g vegan margarine

FOR THE GLAZE
2 tbsp almond milk
2 tbsp maple syrup

In a bowl, mix the almond milk with 45 ml of warm water. Sprinkle the yeast over the surface and leave to activate for 5 minutes, then stir to dissolve. Melt the coconut oil.

Combine the flour, sugar, cardamom and salt in the bowl of a food processor or in a large bowl. Add the milk and yeast mixture and then the coconut oil. With a food processor: knead with a hook attachment until the dough is smooth and elastic and no longer sticky. This may take 5-8 minutes. By hand: mix in the ingredients with a spatula, then place the dough on a floured worktop and knead by hand for at least 10 minutes until smooth and no longer sticky.

Roll the dough into a ball and place in an oiled bowl. Cover with a tea towel. Leave the bowl in a warm place and leave the dough to rise for about 1 hour and 30 minutes, or until doubled in volume.

Preheat the oven to 180°C (gas mark 4). In a bowl, combine the coconut sugar and cinnamon. Take the margarine out of the fridge to soften.

On a floured worktop, roll the dough into a rectangle approximately 40 × 20 cm. Brush with margarine and sprinkle the entire surface with the sugar-cinnamon mixture. Cut strips 4 cm wide lengthwise and roll them up loosely. Place the rolls on a baking tray lined with parchment paper, cover with a tea towel and leave to rise for about 45 minutes in a warm place.

Make the glaze by mixing the almond milk and maple syrup in a bowl. Brush the rolls with the glaze before putting them in the oven for 15 minutes. Brush them again and bake for another 3 minutes, until golden brown. Leave to cool a few minutes before serving.

CHOCOLATE CHIP AND COCONUT MACATIAS

During a stay in Réunion, my mother introduced me to this delicious little brioche with a soft, sweet crumb that she used to enjoy as a child. I was immediately taken by their tastiness and simplicity. Every bakery has them and the locals still eat them for breakfast or as a snack. They come in many flavours, but my favourite is the chocolate chip macatia with a coconut centre.

MAKES 10 MACATIAS
PREP TIME: 30 MINUTES
RESTING TIME: 2 HOURS
BAKING TIME: 15 MINUTES

FOR THE DOUGH
12 g dried baker's yeast
500 g T55 flour
60 g coconut sugar
5 g salt
30 g vegan margarine

FOR DECORATION
150 g desiccated coconut
4 tbsp maple syrup
1 pinch fleur de sel
80 g chocolate chips or chopped
  chocolate

Pour a little warm water into a small bowl. Sprinkle the yeast over the surface and leave for 5 minutes to activate. When the mixture is frothy, stir to dissolve.

Combine the flour, sugar and salt in the bowl of a food processor or in a large bowl. Make a well in the centre and pour in the water and yeast mixture. Gradually add 260 ml of lukewarm water while stirring. Add the softened margarine and mix. Using a food processor: fit with a dough hook and knead the dough until smooth and elastic and no longer sticky. This may take 5-8 minutes. By hand: mix in the ingredients with a spatula, then place the dough on a floured worktop and knead by hand for at least 10 minutes until smooth and no longer sticky.

Roll the dough into a ball and place in an oiled bowl. Cover with a tea towel. Place the bowl in a warm place and leave the dough to rise for about 1 hour, or until doubled in volume.

Whiz the desiccated coconut, maple syrup and salt in a blender until you have a compact, slightly sticky cream.

Place the dough on a floured worktop, add the chocolate chips and knead briefly to distribute them evenly throughout the dough but without overworking it. Divide the dough into 10 equal portions. Shape the dough into small balls and flatten into round discs. Place a dollop of the coconut cream in the centre of each disc, fold over the edges and roll between your hands to form balls. Transfer to a baking tray lined with parchment paper. Cover with a tea towel and leave to rise for 1 hour.

Preheat the oven to 190°C (gas mark 5).

When the macatias have puffed up, put them in the oven for 13–15 minutes, until golden. Make sure that the tops don't brown too much. Leave to cool for a few minutes before eating while still warm and soft.

DANISH PASTRIES FILLED WITH CREAM AND RASPBERRIES

Danish pastries are made with puff pastry, often filled with cream and brushed with a sugar glaze. Although they look simple, they've become a delicacy that has conquered the whole world no matter if they are rolled, plaited, knotted, and filled with jam, fruit or nuts. This is my gluten-free version with cream, raspberries and pistachios.

GLUTEN-FREE

MAKES 6 PASTRIES
PREP TIME: 30 MINUTES
RESTING TIME: 5 HOURS
BAKING TIME: 20 MINUTES

FOR THE CREAM
20 g cornflour
225 ml coconut milk
3 tbsp maple syrup
50 ml lemon juice
1 tsp lemon zest
½ tsp ground vanilla
¼ tsp ground cardamom
1 pinch salt

FOR THE PASTRY
170 g white rice flour
70 g tapioca flour
60 g maize flour
60 g cornflour
60 g coconut sugar
1 heaped tbsp baking powder
¼ tsp salt
200 ml plain soy milk
3 tbsp neutral oil (sunflower, grapeseed, etc.)

FOR THE GLAZE
6 tbsp plain soy milk
1 tbsp maple syrup
4 tbsp coconut sugar

FOR DECORATION
150 g fresh raspberries
40 g pistachios
Zest 1 lemon

Dissolve the cornflour in a little coconut milk. To make the cream, pour the mixture into a saucepan and add the remaining milk and the other ingredients. Bring to the boil, then reduce the heat to medium and cook for 5 minutes, whisking constantly until thickened. Pour the cream into a bowl, leave to cool, then cover with cling film in direct contact and set aside in the fridge for 5 hours.

Preheat the oven to 180°C (gas mark 4) and line a baking tray with parchment paper.

Combine the flours, cornflour, sugar, baking powder and salt in a bowl. Make a well in the middle and pour in the soy milk and oil. Mix to a smooth, non-sticky, malleable dough. Divide the dough into 6 equal portions and shape into balls. Place the balls on the baking tray and flatten them, trying to hollow out the centre and keeping the edges thicker.

Mix the soy milk and maple syrup in a small bowl. Brush the pastry discs with the glaze, then sprinkle sugar over the edges. Bake for 12 minutes, until nice and golden. Remove from the oven and brush again with the glaze. Leave to cool completely.

Stir the cream to make it smooth again. Fill the hollows of the pastries with the cream, then top with the raspberries, crushed pistachios and lemon zest.

FLUFFY PANCAKES AND MISO CARAMEL

Few things are more comforting than a stack of fluffy pancakes for breakfast! Found all over the world, both sweet and savoury, we love eating them at any age and at any time. By the way, did you know that pancakes were first consumed tens of thousands of years ago? Initially in the form of thick cereal galettes, they gradually evolved into what we know today. To continue the story, here's my version.

GLUTEN-FREE

MAKES 8 PANCAKES
PREP TIME: 20 MINUTES
SOAKING TIME: 20 MINUTES
COOKING TIME: 25 MINUTES

FOR THE MISO CARAMEL
6 soft dates
4 tbsp coconut milk
1 tsp vanilla extract
½ tsp brown miso
Pinch fleur de sel

FOR THE PANCAKES
130 g oat flour
30 g ground almonds
10 g cornflour
15 g coconut sugar
1 heaped tbsp baking powder
¼ tsp salt
160 g plain soy yoghurt
140 ml plain non-dairy milk
 (almond or soy)
30 g almond butter
1 tsp vanilla extract
Neutral oil

Soak the dates in hot water for 20 minutes before stoning. Put in a blender with the remaining caramel ingredients. Whiz until smooth and lump-free. If necessary, add a little water to obtain the desired consistency. Set aside in the fridge.

Combine the oat flour, ground almonds, cornflour, sugar, baking powder and salt in a large bowl.

Mix the yoghurt, milk, almond butter and vanilla in a separate bowl to a smooth cream. Pour the mixture into the dry ingredients and mix until the batter is fluid and lump-free. For the pancakes to be light and fluffy, don't overwork the batter. It should be quite thick but still easy to pour. If it's too thick, add a little milk. If it's too liquid, add a little flour.

Heat a lightly oiled non-stick frying pan over medium heat. Pour in a ladleful of batter and spread it out with the back of a spoon to form a disc. Cook until bubbles form on the surface, then carefully flip the pancake over and cook the other side for 2 minutes. Repeat with the rest of the batter. This recipe makes 8 medium-sized pancakes.

Serve the pancakes immediately, generously drizzled with the sauce.

COCOA SMOOTHIE BOWL AND MINI CEREAL COOKIES

This is simply my favourite breakfast! A big bowl of luscious chocolate smoothie, crunchy mini cookies, some fresh fruit and a generous dollop of peanut butter. This simple combination is like a return to your childhood and enjoying comfort food.

GLUTEN-FREE

SERVES 1
PREP TIME: 20 MINUTES
BAKING TIME: 10 MINUTES

FOR THE MINI COOKIES
1¼ tbsp coconut oil
30 g oat flake flour
30 g ground almonds
½ tsp cinnamon
1 pinch salt
3 tsp maple syrup
1 tbsp cacao nibs

FOR THE SMOOTHIE
1 banana
1 large soft date
1 tbsp cocoa powder
½ tsp cinnamon
100 ml coconut milk

FOR DECORATION
½ banana
1 tbsp peanut butter

Preheat the oven to 180°C (gas mark 4) and line a baking tray with parchment paper. Melt the coconut oil.

Mix the oat flour, ground almonds, cinnamon and salt in a bowl. Add the maple syrup and coconut oil and mix to a smooth, slightly sticky dough. Chop the cacao nibs and add to the dough. Use your hands to roll the dough into small balls. Place the balls on a baking tray and press gently with your palm to flatten them slightly. Bake for 10 minutes and leave to cool completely on the baking tray.

Peel the banana. Pit and chop the date. Place all the smoothie ingredients in a blender and whiz at full power until perfectly smooth.

Pour the smoothie into a bowl and top with the mini cookies, pieces of banana and the peanut butter. Eat immediately.

sweet potato smoothie bowl and tropical toasted granola

This is a colourful, vitamin-packed breakfast that will brighten up your day. As well as being delicious, this creamy smoothie is packed with antioxidants and anti-inflammatory ingredients to protect your body in winter. Enjoy with a crunchy granola inspired by the fruity tropical flavours of Bali.

GLUTEN-FREE / OIL-FREE

**SERVES 1 (MAKES 1 JAR OF
 GRANOLA)**
PREP TIME: 20 MINUTES
COOKING TIME: 20 MINUTES

FOR THE SMOOTHIE
150 g sweet potato (about ½
 potato)
1 cm fresh ginger
½ orange
½ tsp turmeric
1–2 tbsp maple syrup
100 ml almond milk

FOR THE GRANOLA
60 g rolled oats
20 g peanuts
15 g coconut chips (or desiccated
 coconut)
½ tsp ground ginger
1 pinch salt
1 tbsp maple syrup
1 tsp vanilla extract
10 g dried goji berries
10 g dried pineapple
10 g dried mango

FOR DECORATION
Coconut yoghurt
Fresh fruit

Peel and dice the sweet potato. Cook in boiling water for 15–20 minutes until tender.

Heat a dry frying pan and toast the oats and peanuts for 2 minutes. Reduce the heat to low and add the coconut, ginger and salt. Toast for 1 minute, stirring regularly. Stir in the maple syrup and vanilla and cook for 2 minutes. Add the diced dried fruit. Spread the granola in a thin layer on a plate and leave to cool completely.

Peel and dice the fresh ginger. Place the drained sweet potato, ginger, orange segments, turmeric, maple syrup and almond milk in a blender and whiz until smooth. Taste and add more maple syrup if necessary.

Pour the smoothie into a bowl and top with granola, 1 tablespoon of coconut yoghurt and fresh fruit. Eat immediately.

CRUNCHY NUT AND CHOCOLATE GRANOLA

There's something magical about that timeless moment when you get up on a Sunday and make a batch of granola in the peace and quiet of the early morning. Toasted cereals and warm spices bring a wonderful aroma to the kitchen, promising a flavoursome and comforting breakfast. If you haven't yet experienced this pleasure, I hope I've convinced you to try it! Not only is it very easy but it's also excellent: I bet you'll never go back to shop-bought granola after this.

GLUTEN-FREE

**MAKES 1 LARGE JAR
 (ABOUT 6 SERVINGS)
PREP TIME: 10 MINUTES
BAKING TIME: 30 MINUTES
RESTING TIME: 1 HOUR**

40 g hazelnuts
40 g almonds
30 g dark chocolate
100 g rolled oats
20 g pumpkin seeds
10 g ground almonds (or another
 kind)
1 tsp cinnamon
1 pinch salt
4 tbsp maple syrup
2 scant tbsp coconut oil
1 tsp vanilla extract

Preheat the oven to 150°C (gas mark 2) and line a baking tray with parchment paper.

Coarsely crush half of the hazelnuts and almonds. Chop the chocolate into pieces. Melt the coconut oil.

Combine the rolled oats, whole and chopped hazelnuts and almonds, pumpkin seeds, flour, cinnamon and salt in a large bowl. Add the maple syrup, coconut oil and vanilla and mix with a spatula. Spread the mixture on the baking tray with a spatula or with your hands to form an even rectangle.

Bake for 30 minutes, until the granola is nice and golden. Keep a careful eye on it during the last few minutes to prevent it burning. Do not mix the granola at this point. Remove it from the oven and immediately add the chopped chocolate, scattering it evenly but without stirring. Leave to cool completely on the baking tray for about 1 hour. Wait until the granola is dry and hard, then break it into nuggets.

TIPS AND VARIATIONS
- To get big, crunchy nuggets, it's very important not to handle the granola until it's completely cool.
- This is a good basic recipe you can adapt as you like and depending on the ingredients at hand. For example, you can use pecans, cashews, sunflower seeds, coconut, and add spices (ginger, cardamom, etc.) or dried fruit after it's been baked. Let your imagination run wild!

CREAMY PORRIDGE, ROASTED APPLES AND CARAMEL

Who said porridge was bland and boring? This rich creamy oatmeal porridge, topped with silky apples and a homemade caramel sauce, is sure to change your mind! It's the ultimate nourishing comfort breakfast. My secret for an incredibly creamy and light texture? Soaking the oats overnight. This makes them more digestible and shortens the cooking time.

GLUTEN-FREE / OIL-FREE

SERVES 2
PREP TIME: 20 MINUTES
SOAKING TIME: OVERNIGHT
COOKING TIME: 10 MINUTES

FOR THE PORRIDGE
75 g rolled oats
300 ml almond milk
½ tsp cinnamon
1 pinch salt
2 tbsp maple syrup
1 tbsp almond butter
1 tsp vanilla extract

FOR THE ROASTED APPLES
1 apple
2 tbsp cider vinegar

FOR THE CARAMEL SAUCE
2 tbsp almond butter
2 tbsp maple syrup
1 tsp vanilla extract

FOR DECORATION
Crunchy nut and chocolate
  granola (see recipe p. 48)
Non-dairy yoghurt

The previous day, mix the oats and milk in a saucepan with 150 ml of water. Leave to soak overnight.

The next morning, bring the mixture to the boil, then lower the heat to very low and cook for 8–10 minutes, stirring regularly. When it becomes creamy, stir in the cinnamon, salt, maple syrup, almond butter and vanilla. Remove the saucepan from the hob and cover.

Wash and dice the apple. Heat a dry frying pan and cook for 5 minutes over medium heat. When the apples are tender and have browned slightly, add the vinegar and cook for a few minutes until it has evaporated.

Mix all the ingredients for the caramel sauce in a small bowl.

Serve the porridge warm with roasted apples, 1 spoonful of yoghurt and 1 handful of granola. Pour the sauce over the top.

TIPS AND VARIATIONS
I recommend soaking the oats to soften them as this will result in a light, creamy and easily digestible porridge. However, this step is optional and you can prepare it the same day. If you make it on the same day the cooking time will be longer.

FRENCH TOAST ROLLED LIKE CHURROS

Who hasn't nibbled on churros at a funfair, at the beach or at a Christmas market? But why not enjoy them at any time? It's believed that churros were brought to Europe centuries ago by Portuguese merchants who had come across them in China... Cuisine is indeed a reflection of cultures from all over the world. Here's a very simple version that combines two great classics, French toast and churros, then dipped in a delicious homemade chocolate sauce. Enjoy! You'll be licking your fingers afterwards.

MAKES 10 ROLLS
PREP TIME: 20 MINUTES
COOKING TIME: 10 MINUTES

FOR THE FRENCH TOAST
10 slices sandwich bread
150 ml soy milk
10 g ground flaxseeds
3 tbsp maple syrup
1 tsp vanilla extract
20 g coconut sugar
30 g desiccated coconut
1 tsp cinnamon
coconut oil or neutral oil

FOR THE CHOCOLATE SAUCE
60 g dark chocolate
100 ml almond milk
1 tbsp maple syrup
1 tbsp non-dairy cream

Remove the crusts from the bread before flattening them with a rolling pin.

Mix the milk and flaxseeds in a bowl. Leave the mixture to thicken for 5 minutes, then add the maple syrup and vanilla. Combine the sugar and desiccated coconut on a flat plate.

Brush one side of each slice with the milk and flaxseed mixture and sprinkle half of the cinnamon all over. Roll the slices up tightly. Dip the rolls in the milk and flaxseed mixture, then roll in the sugar and coconut mixture to coat completely.

Heat a little oil in a frying pan and brown the rolls for 4–5 minutes, turning them regularly until browned all over. Place the rolls on a plate lined with kitchen paper and sprinkle with the remaining cinnamon.

Chop the chocolate before putting it into a small saucepan with the almond milk. Heat gently, stirring to melt. Remove the saucepan from the hob and add the maple syrup and cream. Leave to cool for a few minutes.

Enjoy the rolls dipped in the chocolate sauce.

TIPS AND VARIATIONS
- You can use any type of sandwich bread to make this recipe. White bread is softer and less brittle, but you can also use wholemeal, seed or gluten-free bread if you prefer.
- For even more deliciousness, spread the slices with peanut butter or homemade chocolate spread (see recipe p. 54) before rolling.

SWEET POTATO TOAST, CHOCOLATE SPREAD AND HOMEMADE JAM

If I say 'French breakfast' to you, you'll probably answer: 'Toast'! Definitely not a cliché, toast with butter and jam is still a staple on French tables and has left an indelible mark on our culture. If you're a bit tired of good old toast, here's a surprising version that's sure to please: sweet potato toast, spread generously with jam, peanut butter and homemade chocolate spread! With no refined sugar and naturally gluten-free, it's still very satisfying.

GLUTEN-FREE

MAKES 4 SLICES, 1 SMALL JAR OF JAM AND 1 SMALL JAR OF SPREAD
PREP TIME: 20 MINUTES
RESTING TIME: 30 MINUTES
COOKING TIME: 20 MINUTES

FOR THE JAM
200 g fresh or frozen berries
30 g chia seeds
1–2 tbsp maple syrup
1 tbsp lemon juice

FOR THE SPREAD
80 g tinned kidney beans
4 large dates
40 g hazelnut butter
20 g unsweetened cocoa
1 pinch salt
40 ml non-dairy milk

FOR THE TOAST
1 large sweet potato (preferably organic)
Peanut butter (optional)

Put the berries into a small saucepan. Cook for 5 minutes over medium heat to soften completely before mashing with a fork. Remove the saucepan from the hob, add the chia seeds, maple syrup and lemon juice and stir. Pour into a jar and refrigerate for 30 minutes to thicken.

Rinse and drain the beans. Soak the dates in hot water for 20 minutes to soften. Pit and chop the dates before whizzing in a food processor with the beans to make a thick paste. Add the hazelnut butter, cocoa and salt and whiz again. While whizzing, gradually add the milk until you have a spreadable consistency. Transfer to a jar and set aside in the fridge.

Wash and dry the sweet potato thoroughly. If it's organic, leave the skin on, otherwise peel it. Cut lengthwise into regular slices about 6 mm thick.

In a toaster: toast the sweet potato slices on the highest setting as many times as necessary to ensure they are cooked through, tender and slightly browned. Take care they don't burn! In the oven: lightly brush the slices with oil and arrange on a baking tray lined with parchment paper. Bake at 190°C (gas mark 5) for 12–15 minutes, until tender and browned.

Spread the toast with spreads of your choice. The jam is good with peanut butter.

TIPS AND VARIATIONS
Berries (raspberries, blueberries, blackberries, redcurrants, strawberries, etc.), fresh or frozen, are particularly suitable for making chia-seed jam, but you can also use other fruit (figs, plums, apricots, etc.), which simply need to be cooked a little longer.

SOFT COOKIeS WITH SeeDS AND DRIeD FRUIT

Cookies for breakfast? Absolutely! Everything goes with these delicious biscuits. This version is high in fibre, has no refined sugar and is satisfying: it's one of my favourite recipes for a healthy, nourishing and very flavoursome breakfast or snack. Easy to store or to eat on the go, they're ideal for snacking at work, while enjoying outdoor activities, on the road, for a picnic or for when you go camping.

GLUTEN-FREE

MAKES 8
PREP TIME: 10 MINUTES
COOKING TIME: 12 MINUTES

4 tbsp coconut oil
100 g rolled oats
60 g oat flour
50 g ground almonds
1½ tsp baking powder
1 tsp cinnamon
1 pinch salt
80 g almond butter
3 tbsp maple syrup
30 g coconut sugar
1 tsp vanilla extract
20 g pumpkin seeds
20 g walnuts, chopped
20 g dried cranberries
30 g dried apricots, chopped
30 g dark chocolate chips

Preheat the oven to 180°C (gas mark 4) and line a baking tray with parchment paper. Melt the coconut oil.

Combine the rolled oats, oat flour, ground almonds, baking powder, cinnamon and salt in a bowl.

Mix the almond butter, coconut oil, maple syrup, sugar and vanilla in a separate bowl until smooth. Pour into the dry ingredients and mix again: the dough should be smooth, slightly dry and crumbly but firm enough to work with. Stir in the pumpkin seeds, nuts, cranberries, apricots and chocolate chips.

Shape the dough into 8 balls by rolling and compacting them firmly with your hands. Place the balls on a baking tray and gently flatten. The dough will not spread out during baking, so it's important to shape the cookies well at this point.

Bake for 12 minutes, until nice and golden. Leave to cool on the baking tray. Be careful not to touch the cookies when they come out of the oven as they're very fragile, but will harden as they cool.

SAVOURY ENGLISH BREAKFAST PORRIDGE

For a long time, the idea of a savoury breakfast didn't appeal to me. So, when I went to Scotland to study, I wasn't exactly enamoured by the idea of the traditional English breakfast. Beans, mushrooms and spinach for breakfast? Just a little for me, please! But that was before trying and discovering a tasty nutritious dish... Whether you're already a fan of savoury breakfasts or you have a sweet tooth, this reinterpretation – in the guise of a creamy courgette porridge – might very well convince you to go *British*.

GLUTEN-FREE

SERVES 2
PREP TIME: 25 MINUTES
COOKING TIME: 20 MINUTES

FOR THE ROASTED CHERRY TOMATOES
10 cherry tomatoes
1 tbsp olive oil
2 tsp balsamic vinegar
1 pinch salt

FOR THE PORRIDGE
120 g courgette
50 g rolled oats
50 g tinned white beans
2 handfuls fresh spinach
½ tsp garlic powder
½ tsp cumin
Salt and pepper

FOR THE PAN-FRIED MUSHROOMS
120 g white mushrooms
2 tbsp soy sauce
½ garlic clove
½ tsp fresh or dried thyme
½ tsp dried oregano
1 tbsp olive oil
Salt and pepper

FOR THE GRILLED CORN
50 g tinned sweetcorn kernels
1 tbsp olive oil
Salt

FOR DECORATION
Plain non-dairy yoghurt
Fresh chives, chopped
Pepper

Preheat the oven to 180°C (gas mark 4).

Arrange the tomatoes in a shallow oven-proof dish. Add the oil, vinegar and salt and toss to coat. Bake for 20 minutes, until they begin to wrinkle.

Grate the courgette, keeping the skin on if it's organic. Combine the rolled oats and grated courgette in a saucepan with 250 ml of water. Bring to the boil, then reduce the heat to very low and simmer for about 8 minutes, stirring regularly. When the porridge is creamy, add the rinsed and drained white beans, spinach, garlic and cumin, and season with salt and pepper. Cook for 2 minutes, then remove the saucepan from the hob and cover.

Wash the mushrooms and coarsely chop. Crush the garlic and mix with the soy sauce, thyme and oregano in a bowl, add the mushrooms and marinate for 5 minutes. Heat the oil in a frying pan. Add the mushrooms along with the marinade and fry for 5 minutes over high heat, stirring occasionally. Season to taste.

Drain the sweetcorn and fry for 3–4 minutes in a frying pan with the oil. Season with salt.

Serve the porridge warm with the roasted cherry tomatoes, mushrooms, pan-fried corn and 1 spoonful of yoghurt. Sprinkle with the chives and add a turn of the pepper mill.

PRETZEL BURGERS, VEGETABLE PATTIES AND SCRAMBLED CHICKPEAS

The great thing about burgers is that there are no actual rules. So why not have them for breakfast? With a soft pretzel, root vegetable patty and scrambled chickpeas, these tasty little burgers are ideal for both brunch and lunch.

MAKES 4 SMALL BURGERS
PREP TIME: 40 MINUTES
RESTING TIME: 1 HOUR 30 MINUTES
COOKING TIME: 30 MINUTES

FOR THE PRETZEL DOUGH
75 ml plain soy milk
10 g fresh baker's yeast (or 5 g dry yeast)
260 g T65 wheat flour
6 g salt
40 ml neutral oil
100 g bicarbonate of soda
1 tbsp salt

FOR THE VEGETABLE PATTIES
100 g sweet potato
100 g parsnips
60 g carrot
1 yellow onion
60 g chickpea flour
Salt and pepper
Olive oil

FOR THE SCRAMBLED CHICKPEAS
50 g chickpea flour
2 tbsp nutritional yeast
1 tbsp mustard
½ tsp turmeric
1 tsp garlic powder
1 pinch kala namak salt
130 ml plain non-dairy milk
Olive oil

FOR THE SAUCE
80 g thick non-dairy yoghurt
20 g tomato paste
2 tsp maple syrup
1 tbsp soy sauce
1 tbsp balsamic vinegar
1 tsp garlic powder
1 tsp smoked paprika
1 pinch salt

FOR DECORATION
Baby spinach leaves

Mix the soy milk with 75 ml of warm water. Crumble the yeast over it and leave for 5 minutes to activate, then stir to dissolve.

Combine the flour and salt in the bowl of a food processor or in a large bowl. Make a well in the centre and pour in the oil and the water, milk and yeast mixture. Knead in a food processor with the hook attachment or by hand on a floured worktop for 8–10 minutes, until the dough is smooth and no longer sticky. Roll the dough into a ball and place it in an oiled bowl. Cover with a tea towel. Place the bowl in a warm place and leave the dough to rise for about 1 hour, or until doubled in volume. Flour the worktop and divide the dough into 4 equal portions, then shape into balls. Place the dough balls on a baking tray lined with parchment paper, cover with a tea towel and leave to rest for 30 minutes.

Preheat the oven to 200°C (gas mark 6). Boil 1 litre of water with the bicarbonate and salt in a large saucepan. Dip the dough balls one by one into the boiling water with a skimmer and poach for 30 seconds. Drain each one and place on another baking tray. Bake for 20 minutes and leave to cool for a few moments on a rack.

Peel and grate the sweet potato, parsnip and carrot. Peel and chop the onion. Put the grated vegetables in a bowl, add the chickpea flour, season and mix until it comes together well. Place 4 heaped spoonfuls of the batter in a heated and oiled frying pan. Brown the patties for 3 minutes on each side.

Combine the chickpea flour, yeast, mustard, turmeric, garlic and salt in a bowl. Add the milk and mix to obtain a smooth lump-free batter. Heat a little oil in a large frying pan. Pour the mixture into the hot frying pan and cook for 1 minute. When it starts to thicken, stir with a spatula to break it up and cook for a further 2 minutes.

Mix all the ingredients for the sauce in a bowl. Cut the pretzel rolls in half. Brush the top of the bottom half with sauce, then place a vegetable patty, some spinach leaves and scrambled chickpeas on top. Add sauce and top with the other half of the pretzel roll.

PEANUT HUMMUS AND SHIITAKE MUSHROOMS

Hummus is an essential part of plant-based cooking. And for good reason: this typical Middle Eastern and Mediterranean dish is not only delicious and easy to prepare, but also high in protein. If you're already familiar with traditional hummus, made of chickpeas and tahini, wait until you discover this surprising version made with white beans and peanut butter. Spread it on toast or use it as an ingredient in a range of dishes.

GLUTEN-FREE OPTION

MAKES 2 SLICES
PREP TIME: 20 MINUTES
COOKING TIME: 20 MINUTES

FOR THE ROASTED CHERRY TOMATOES
10 cherry tomatoes
1 tbsp olive oil
2 tsp balsamic vinegar
1 pinch salt

FOR THE PAN-FRIED SHIITAKES
50 g shiitakes
3 tbsp soy sauce
1 tsp maple syrup
½ garlic clove
1 cm fresh ginger
1 tbsp coconut oil

FOR THE HUMMUS
150 g tinned white beans
30 g peanut butter
1 tbsp plain non-dairy yoghurt
1 tbsp lemon juice
½ tsp garlic powder
½ tsp ground paprika
1 pinch salt

FOR THE TOAST
2 slices bread (gluten-free if necessary)
1 handful toasted pine nuts
Rocket leaves
Dash of balsamic vinegar

Preheat the oven to 180°C (gas mark 4). Arrange the tomatoes in a shallow oven-proof dish. Pour the oil and vinegar over them, sprinkle with salt and toss to coat well. Bake for 20 minutes, until they begin to wrinkle.

Clean and gently dry the shiitakes. Remove the stems and cut the mushrooms into strips.

Finely chop the garlic and grate the ginger, then mix with the soy sauce and maple syrup in a bowl.

Heat the coconut oil in a frying pan and sauté the shiitakes for 8 minutes over high heat, stirring regularly. Add the sauce and cook for another 5 minutes, stirring. Remove the frying pan from the hob.

Place the drained and rinsed beans and all the other hummus ingredients in a blender or food processor and whiz until smooth and creamy. Taste and adjust the seasoning.

Toast the bread, spread with the hummus and top with the tomatoes and shiitake mushrooms. Add pine nuts, rocket leaves and drizzle with balsamic vinegar before serving.

SANDWICHES

TOMATO PAN-BAGNAT AND CRUSHED CHICKPEAS

Pan-bagnat, nicknamed 'poor-man's food', is often made with simple ingredients, but is packed with flavour. This sandwich from Nice consists of a round loaf of bread stuffed with fresh, local and seasonal ingredients: peppers, olives, tomatoes, basil, olive oil, and sometimes anchovies and tuna. This is my recipe for pan-bagnat with homemade rolls flavoured with tomato and crushed chickpeas with a briny flavour.

MAKES 4 SANDWICHES
PREP TIME: 20 MINUTES
RESTING TIME: 1 HOUR 40 MINUTES
COOKING TIME: 20 MINUTES

FOR THE TOMATO ROLLS
12 g fresh baker's yeast (or 6 g dry yeast)
300 g T65 flour
5 g salt
45 g tomato paste
6 sprigs fresh thyme
45 g dried tomatoes

FOR THE CRUSHED CHICKPEAS
2 shallots
10 g capers
4 sprigs dill
260 g cooked chickpeas
½ sheet nori seaweed, crumbled
2 tbsp mustard
2 tbsp olive oil
1 tbsp capers in brine or vinegar
2 tsp maple syrup
1 pinch ground black pepper
1 pinch kala namak salt

FOR DECORATION
2 tomatoes
1 cucumber
8 black olives
Dill

Crumble the yeast into 180 ml of warm water and leave to activate for 5 minutes, then stir to dissolve.

Combine the flour and salt in a bowl or in the bowl of a food processor. Stir in the water and yeast mixture. Add the tomato paste, thyme and dried tomatoes. Knead in a food processor with the hook attachment or by hand on a floured worktop for 8–10 minutes, until the dough is smooth and elastic. Roll the dough into a ball and place in an oiled bowl. Cover with a tea towel and leave the dough to rise in a warm place for 1 hour, or until doubled in volume.

Divide the dough into 4 equal portions and shape into small balls. Place the balls on a baking tray lined with parchment paper, cover again and leave to rise for a further 40 minutes.

Peel and chop the shallots, capers and dill. Rinse and drain the chickpeas, then crush with a fork. Add the shallots, capers, dill, nori seaweed and the remaining ingredients. Mix to a creamy consistency. Taste and adjust the seasoning. Cover with cling film in direct contact and refrigerate.

Preheat the oven to 230°C (gas mark 8). Slice the tomatoes and the cucumber. Pit the olives and cut in half.

Bake the rolls for 20 minutes until golden brown, then leave to cool on a wire rack. Cut the rolls in half and spread with crushed chickpeas, then add the sliced tomato and cucumber, a few olives and dill.

TIPS AND VARIATIONS
Nothing beats the freshness of just-baked homemade bread. You can, of course, use ready-made rolls or any of the homemade bread recipes in this book. Burger buns, pita bread, wraps, sandwich bread... There's lots to choose from!
These briny-flavoured crushed chickpeas can also be added to cold salads, mixed with rice or pasta with a few vegetables, olives and corn. Perfect for a summer lunch or picnic.

BAGUETTE SANDWICH WITH MARINATED TOFU, PESTO AND GRILLED PEPPER

Basil, olive oil, grilled peppers and Provençal herbs; these are the flavours that smell of the South of France and the sun! Fresh, local and seasonal ingredients and authentic tastes for a truly flavour-laden sandwich. Take it with you on your lunch break when you feel you need to escape for a moment.

MAKES 2 SANDWICHES
PREP TIME: 20 MINUTES
RESTING TIME: 3 HOURS
COOKING TIME: 20 MINUTES

FOR THE MARINATED TOFU
100 g plain firm tofu
2 tbsp olive oil
2 tbsp cider vinegar
1 tbsp nutritional yeast
½ garlic clove, crushed
1 tsp dried oregano
¼ tsp salt

FOR THE GRILLED PEPPER
1 red pepper
1 tbsp olive oil
1 tsp herbs de Provence
1 pinch salt

FOR THE PESTO
20 g fresh basil
½ garlic clove, crushed
70 g pine nuts
3 tbsp nutritional yeast
2 tbsp olive oil
1 tbsp lemon juice
Salt and pepper

FOR DECORATION
1 baguette
8 black olives
2 handfuls rocket leaves

Press the tofu with kitchen paper to remove as much water as possible and cut into long slices about 5 mm thick.

Mix the oil, vinegar, yeast, garlic, oregano and salt in a shallow dish. Place the tofu slices in the marinade and toss to coat. Leave in the fridge for at least 3 hours (ideally overnight).

Preheat the oven to 200°C (gas mark 6).

Wash, dry and seed the pepper, then cut into long slices. Transfer, skin side up, to a baking tray lined with parchment paper. Drizzle with oil, sprinkle with herbs de Provence and salt, and toss with your hands to coat the pepper. Roast for 20 minutes until the skin of the pepper wrinkles and brown spots appear. Leave to cool in the oven.

Chop the basil and garlic clove and place all the ingredients for the pesto in a blender or food processor. Whiz to a smooth but still slightly grainy texture. Taste and adjust the seasoning.

Cut the baguette in half and then slice each half lengthwise. Pit the olives and cut into slices. Spread pesto on both halves of the bread before topping with slices of marinated tofu, grilled pepper, rocket leaves and olives, then close the sandwich.

TIPS AND VARIATIONS
- Marinated tofu is very easy to make and can be used like feta cheese in many dishes. Cut into cubes, it can be added to a tomato, cucumber, black olive and watermelon salad; it can also be crumbled over grilled vegetables, chachouka, pasta or any dish with Provençal flavours.
- Basil pesto is a basic ingredient to have in your fridge at all times. It's excellent for seasoning and spicing up a pasta dish, risotto or simply spread on toast for a snack.

THE ULTIMATE CHEESE BURGER

There's no need to introduce you to the star of American street food and the emblem of the country's culture and fast food: the hamburger. As the name suggests, this famous sandwich originated in Hamburg, Germany, before crossing the Atlantic and conquering the world. The French and the Brits are no exception to this trend, but the French are the biggest consumers of burgers in Europe! I'm hoping to do burgers justice with this 100% homemade version featuring soft buns, a vegetable patty, grilled rice bacon slices, onion pickles and a melting cheese sauce.

MAKES 4 BURGERS
PREP TIME: 1 HOUR
RESTING TIME: 1 HOUR 30 MINUTES
COOKING TIME: 40 MINUTES
SOAKING TIME: 20 MINUTES

FOR THE BURGER BUNS
50 g vegan margarine
12 g fresh baker's yeast (or 6 g dry yeast)
300 g T55 flour
12 g cane sugar
4 g salt
125 ml almond milk
50 ml soy milk
1 tbsp maple syrup
2 tbsp sesame seeds

FOR THE 'PATTIES'
½ yellow onion
240 g brown mushrooms
1 tbsp olive oil
300 g cooked brown rice
240 g tinned kidney beans
1 tbsp soy sauce
½ tsp garlic powder
1 tsp dried thyme
Salt and pepper

FOR THE RICE BACON
4 tbsp soy sauce
2 tbsp olive oil
2 tbsp tomato paste
1 tbsp maple syrup
½ tsp liquid smoke (optional)
1 tsp smoked paprika
4 sheets rice paper

FOR THE ONION PICKLES
1 red onion
30 ml white vinegar
1 tbsp cane sugar
1 tsp coarse salt

FOR THE CHEESE SAUCE
100 g cashew nuts
1 garlic clove
10 g nutritional yeast
100 ml plain non-dairy milk
2 tbsp lemon juice
1 tbsp mustard
1 tsp onion powder
½ tsp smoked paprika
½ tsp turmeric
1 pinch salt

FOR THE BARBECUE SAUCE
40 g tomato paste
2 tbsp soy sauce
2 tbsp cider vinegar

1 tbsp maple syrup
1 tsp garlic powder
1 tsp smoked paprika
½ tsp ground cumin
¼ tsp ground chilli
1 pinch salt

FOR DECORATION
4 lettuce leaves

Melt the margarine. Crumble the yeast over 30 ml of warm water and leave to activate for 5 minutes, then stir to dissolve.

Combine the flour, sugar and salt in the bowl of a food processor or in a bowl. Make a well in the centre and pour in the melted margarine, almond milk and the water and yeast mixture. Knead in a food processor with the hook attachment or by hand on a floured worktop for 8–10 minutes, until the dough is smooth and elastic. Roll the dough into a ball and place in an oiled bowl. Cover with a tea towel and leave the dough to rise in a warm place for 1 hour, or until doubled in volume.

Divide the dough into 4 equal portions and shape into balls. Place the balls on a baking tray lined with parchment paper, cover with a tea towel and leave to rest for a further 30 minutes.

Preheat the oven to 200°C (gas mark 6).

Mix the soy milk and maple syrup in a bowl. Brush the bread with the glaze and sprinkle with sesame seeds. Bake for 15 minutes until golden brown. Brush the loaves again with the glaze before leaving them to cool.

Peel and chop the onion. Wash and dice the mushrooms. Heat the oil in a frying pan and gently fry the onion for 2 minutes, then add the mushrooms and cook for about 5 minutes over medium heat, until they release their water.

Whiz the rice, rinsed and drained beans and the remaining ingredients to a paste. Transfer the paste to a bowl and stir in the cooked onion and mushrooms. It should be firm enough to form the patties. If it's too sticky, add a little flour. Shape into 4 patties about 2–3 cm thick. Heat a non-stick frying pan with a little oil and cook over medium heat for about 5 minutes on each side.

Mix the ingredients for the rice bacon in a bowl, except for the rice paper. Soak the sheets of rice paper in warm water to soften, then place one sheet on top of another, making sure to remove any air bubbles. Repeat with the other two sheets. Brush both sides of the two double sheets with marinade before cutting into strips.

Heat a little oil in a frying pan and fry the strips for a few minutes on each side until crispy. Place on a sheet of kitchen paper and leave to cool.

Peel the onion and cut into thin slices. Combine the vinegar, sugar and salt in a saucepan with 80 ml of water and bring to the boil. Add the onion and leave to cook for 10 minutes. Pour the mixture into a jar with all the pan juices, close and refrigerate.

Soak the cashew nuts in hot water for 20 minutes to soften. Rinse, drain and whiz the nuts with the rest of the cheese sauce ingredients to a creamy consistency.

Prepare the barbecue sauce by mixing all the ingredients in a bowl with 4 tablespoons of water.

Cut the bread in half and toast in a frying pan. Brush the cut sides with barbecue sauce, then place a lettuce leaf, patty, cheese sauce, a few strips of rice bacon and onion pickles on top before closing the burgers.

NAAN STUFFED WITH MASHED PUMPKIN, HAZELNUTS AND CAPERS

Naan is to South Asia what the baguette is to France. It's most often associated with Indian cuisine, but this delicious flatbread is also eaten in other parts of Asia. Today, there's no need to travel to enjoy naan as it features on the menu of no matter which Indian restaurant you go to. Plain, with garlic, with cheese or nuts, there are a thousand ways to prepare it. So why not stuff it with mashed pumpkin, capers and roasted hazelnuts?

FOR 3 STUFFED NAANS
PREP TIME: 30 MINUTES
RESTING TIME: 1 HOUR
COOKING TIME: 25 MINUTES

FOR THE NAAN
6 g dried baker's yeast
300 g T55 flour
1 tbsp cane sugar
1 tsp salt
1 tbsp olive oil
75 g thick non-dairy yoghurt
1 garlic clove, finely chopped
1 tsp dried oregano

FOR THE PUMPKIN PURÉE
200 g butternut squash (or other
  variety)
1 tbsp olive oil
1 pinch salt
20 g thick non-dairy yoghurt
1 tsp dried sage
¼ tsp black pepper
1 pinch ground nutmeg

FOR DECORATION
15 capers
1 handful roasted hazelnuts

Pour 20 ml of warm water into a small bowl. Sprinkle the yeast over it and leave to activate for 5 minutes, then stir to dissolve.

Combine the flour, sugar and salt in a large bowl. Make a well in the centre and pour in the water and yeast mixture, oil and yoghurt. Mix briefly with a spatula. Gradually stir in 70 ml of warm water. Add the finely chopped garlic and oregano and mix again. Place the dough on a lightly floured worktop and knead for at least 6 minutes until smooth, elastic and no longer sticky. If it's too sticky when you finish kneading, add a little flour. Roll the dough into a ball and place in an oiled bowl. Cover with a tea towel, put in a warm place and leave to rise for about 1 hour, or until doubled in volume.

Preheat the oven to 200°C (gas mark 6).

Peel and dice the squash. Place on a baking tray lined with parchment paper, add the oil and salt and toss to coat the squash. Bake for 20 minutes, until the squash turns nice and golden. In a bowl, mash the cooked squash with a fork. Add the yoghurt, sage, pepper and nutmeg. Taste and adjust the seasoning.

Divide the dough into 6 equal portions. Shape the dough into balls and use a rolling pin to flatten to make discs measuring about 15 cm in diameter. Put a dollop of squash purée in the centre of 3 discs and spread it out, leaving a 2 cm border around the edge. Add a few capers and crushed hazelnuts. Top each one with another disc and press the edges lightly to seal.

Heat a lightly oiled non-stick frying pan over high heat, put in a naan and cook for 3 minutes. When the dough begins puffing up, turn the naan over and cook the other side for 2 minutes, or until browned to your liking. Repeat with other naans. Leave to cool for a few moments before enjoying the naan while still warm and soft.

TIPS AND VARIATIONS
- This recipe for stuffed naan can be adapted with whatever filling you like. You can swap the squash purée for any other seasonal vegetable purée, hummus, baba ghanoush, pesto or grated non-dairy cheese.
- You can also make plain naan to serve with dahl, curries, chachouka and other dishes that have a sauce. In that case, simply bake the discs plain, without the filling.

OYSTER MUSHROOM HOT DOGS AND SATAY SAUCE

Have you ever wondered why they're called that? There are several theories, but don't worry, no dogs were mistreated in the story. The word 'dog' is said to be a synonym for 'sausage' perhaps in reference to the elongated body a dachshund has. This special sandwich originated in Germany before ending up in America and becoming a symbol of New York. Via this satay-style hot dog, I've transported it to Indonesia, using a soft brioche bun and roasted oyster mushrooms in peanut sauce.

MAKES 6 HOT DOGS
PREP TIME: 30 MINUTES
RESTING TIME: 1 HOUR 30 MINUTES
COOKING TIME: 20 MINUTES

FOR THE BUNS
50 g vegan margarine, melted
12 g fresh baker's yeast (or 6 g dry yeast)
300 g T55 flour
12 g cane sugar
4 g salt
125 ml almond milk
50 ml soy milk
1 tbsp maple syrup

FOR THE OYSTER MUSHROOMS IN SATAY SAUCE
300 g oyster mushrooms
2 cloves garlic
1 cm fresh ginger
150 g peanut butter
180 ml coconut milk
6 tbsp soy sauce
3 tbsp lime juice
3 tbsp coconut sugar
1 tsp ground cumin
1 tsp ground coriander
1 tbsp coconut oil
1 handful crushed roasted peanuts

FOR THE HOT DOGS
2 lettuce hearts
1 green chilli, sliced
12 gherkins, sliced
2 handfuls fried onions

Crumble or sprinkle the yeast over 30 ml of warm water and leave to activate for 5 minutes, then stir to dissolve.

Combine the flour, sugar and salt in the bowl of a food processor or in a bowl. Make a well and pour in the melted margarine, almond milk and the water and yeast mixture. Knead in a food processor with the hook attachment or by hand on a floured worktop for 8–10 minutes, until the dough is smooth and elastic. Roll the dough into a ball and place in an oiled bowl. Cover with a tea towel and leave the dough to rise in a warm place for 1 hour, or until doubled in volume. Divide the dough into 6 equal portions. Shape into balls and then stretch to make elongated buns. Place the dough on a baking tray lined with parchment paper, cover with a tea towel and leave to rest for a further 30 minutes.

Preheat the oven to 200°C (gas mark 6). Mix the soy milk and maple syrup in a bowl. Brush the buns with the glaze. Bake for 15 minutes until golden brown. Brush again with the glaze before leaving them to cool.

Clean the oyster mushrooms and tear them into pieces by hand. Peel and finely chop the garlic and ginger. Whiz the garlic, ginger, peanut butter, coconut milk, soy sauce, lemon juice, sugar, cumin and coriander with 45 ml of water to make the sauce. Pour the sauce into a bowl and add the torn oyster mushrooms. Mix and leave to marinate in the fridge for at least 1 hour.

Heat the coconut oil in a frying pan. Add the oyster mushrooms and the marinade and cook for 5 minutes, stirring well. Stir in the crushed peanuts.

Chop the lettuce. Slice the chilli and gherkins. Cut the buns in half without opening them completely and fill with lettuce, oyster mushrooms, chilli, pickles and fried onions.

CRUNCHY BÁNH MÌ BURGERS

This *bánh mì* burger is the coming together of the quintessential burger and the most popular sandwich in Vietnam. The word *bánh mì* refers to the baguette in which this sandwich is served with grated pickled vegetables, fresh coriander and a spicy sauce. In this recipe, I've swapped the baguette for a brioche bun.

MAKES 4 BURGERS
PREP TIME: 40 MINUTES
RESTING TIME: 1 HOUR 30
  MINUTES
COOKING TIME: 35 MINUTES
SOAKING TIME: 20 MINUTES

FOR THE BURGER BUNS
50 g vegan margarine, melted
12 g fresh baker's yeast (or 6 g
  dry yeast)
300 g T55 flour
12 g cane sugar
4 g salt
125 ml almond milk
50 ml soy milk
1 tbsp maple syrup
Sesame seeds

FOR THE AUBERGINE FRITTERS
1 small aubergine
50 g white rice flour
20 g cornflour
½ tsp salt
40 g peanut butter
200 g plain cornflakes

FOR THE CUCUMBER PICKLES
1 cucumber, sliced
60 ml white vinegar
1 tsp coarse salt

FOR THE SPICY MAYONNAISE
100 g cashew nuts
120 g coconut milk
1 garlic clove
2 tbsp cider vinegar
2 tbsp mustard
1 tbsp maple syrup
½ tsp ground ginger
¼ tsp ground chilli
1 pinch kala namak salt
1 pinch ground black pepper

FOR DECORATION
2 carrots
1 small bunch coriander, chopped

Crumble or sprinkle the yeast over 30 ml of warm water and leave to activate for 5 minutes, then stir to dissolve. Combine the flour, sugar and salt in the bowl of a food processor or in a bowl. Make a well and pour in the melted margarine, the almond milk and the water and yeast mixture. Knead in a food processor with the hook attachment or by hand on a floured worktop for 8–10 minutes, until the dough is smooth and elastic. Roll the dough into a ball and place in an oiled bowl. Cover with a tea towel and leave the dough to rise in a warm place for 1 hour, or until doubled in volume. Divide the dough into 4 equal portions and shape into balls. Place the balls on a baking tray lined with parchment paper, cover with a tea towel and leave to rest for a further 30 minutes.

Preheat the oven to 200°C (gas mark 6). Mix the soy milk and maple syrup in a bowl. Brush the rolls with the glaze and sprinkle with sesame seeds. Bake for 15 minutes, until golden brown. Brush the loaves again with the glaze before leaving them to cool.

Cut the aubergine into slices about 5 mm thick. Combine the flour, cornflour, salt and peanut butter with 80 ml of water to make a batter. Crumble the cornflakes into a dish. Dip the aubergine slices in the batter to coat and then in the cornflakes. Arrange on a baking tray lined with parchment paper and bake for 20 minutes.

Wash and thinly slice the cucumber. In a jar, mix the vinegar and salt with 150 ml of water. Add the cucumber slices, close the jar and set aside in the fridge.

Soak the cashew nuts in hot water for 20 minutes to soften them. Rinse, drain and whiz the nuts with the remaining mayonnaise ingredients to a creamy sauce.

Peel and grate the carrots. Cut the buns in half and toast in a frying pan. Spread mayonnaise on both halves of the buns, add the grated carrots, aubergine fritters, cucumber pickle and top with chopped coriander.

PITA BREAD STUFFED WITH RED LENTIL FALAFEL

It's impossible to have a cookbook of traditional recipes without one for pita kebab! This quintessential Middle Eastern dish can now be found all around the world. From my student days in Montpellier to my last stay in Istanbul, the kebab capital of the world, it's always been part of my culinary landscape. This version of a street food classic now comes to your kitchen, tastier than ever, stuffed with red lentil falafel.

**MAKES 4 PITA FLATBREADS
(20 FALAFELS)
PREP TIME: 30 MINUTES
RESTING TIME: 1 HOUR 20
MINUTES
COOKING TIME: 35 MINUTES**

FOR THE PITA BREAD
3 g dried baker's yeast
170 g T55 flour
40 g T150 flour
2 tbsp cane sugar
1 tsp salt
2 tsp olive oil

FOR THE FALAFELS (20 PATTIES)
200 g red lentils
1 shallot
160 g chickpea flour
60 g sesame seeds
50 g tomato paste
4 tbsp olive oil
1 tsp smoked paprika
1 tsp cumin
1 tsp garlic powder
¼ tsp salt

FOR THE YOGURT SAUCE
4 sprigs fresh coriander
180 g thick non-dairy yoghurt
3 tbsp lemon juice
3 tbsp olive oil
¼ tsp salt

FOR DECORATION
1 tomato
Rocket leaves

Pour 20 ml of warm water into a small bowl. Sprinkle the yeast over the surface and leave it to activate for 5 minutes, then stir to dissolve.

Combine the flours, sugar and salt in a large bowl. Make a well in the centre and pour in the water and yeast mixture and the oil. Mix briefly, then gradually add 110 ml of warm water while stirring. Place the dough on a lightly floured worktop and knead by hand for at least 6 minutes, until smooth and just slightly sticky. Roll the dough into a ball and place in an oiled bowl. Cover with a tea towel. Place the bowl in a warm place and leave to rise for about 1 hour, until doubled in volume.

Rinse the lentils before cooking in a saucepan of boiling water for 10 minutes, then drain. Peel and finely chop the shallot. Whiz all the ingredients to a thick mixture that is dry enough to shape into balls. If it's too sticky, add a little flour.

Preheat the oven to 180°C (gas mark 4) and line a baking tray with parchment paper. Take 1 spoonful of lentil mixture and shape into a ball. Place the balls on the baking tray and gently press to flatten. Repeat with all 20 balls to make the falafels. Bake for 20 minutes, then leave to cool.

Divide the pita dough into 4 equal portions. Shape the dough into balls and use a rolling pin to flatten to make discs measuring about 15 cm in diameter. Place them on a baking tray lined with parchment paper, cover with a tea towel and leave for 20 minutes. Heat a dry non-stick frying pan over high heat and cook the flatbreads for 2–3 minutes, turning regularly and taking care not to pierce the pita bread.

Finely chop the coriander and mix all the ingredients for the yoghurt sauce. Cut the flatbreads in half. Brush the inside with sauce, then add the falafel, tomato slices and rocket leaves.

MELTED GRILLED CHEESE SANDWICH AND ROASTED PEAR, ROCKET PESTO AND PICKLES

Once upon a time, a grilled cheese or melted cheese sandwich was nothing more than just that. A fair amount of cheese between two slices of buttered bread, toasted for a few minutes in a frying pan, and there you go – a comforting snack just the way you like it and that takes you back to your childhood. Here, I suggest adding a little originality to it with tangy pickles, walnut and rocket pesto and roasted pear slices. A real treat!

MAKES 2 SANDWICHES
PREP TIME: 20 MINUTES
COOKING TIME: 15 MINUTES
RESTING TIME: 24 HOURS

FOR THE PICKLES
50 g red onion, cut into fine slices
50 g pink radishes
50 ml cider vinegar
20 g coconut or cane sugar
10 g salt
1 bay leaf
1 tbsp black peppercorns

FOR THE CHEESE SAUCE
15 g cornflour
180 ml coconut milk
10 g nutritional yeast
1 tbsp caper brine
½ tsp garlic powder
½ tsp onion powder
1 pinch salt

FOR THE PESTO
1 garlic clove
25 g walnuts
30 g rocket
15 g fresh basil
1 tbsp olive oil
1 tbsp lemon juice
1 tsp balsamic vinegar
Salt and pepper

FOR THE SANDWICH
1 pear
4 slices bread (sandwich or
  farmhouse)
Vegan margarine
1 handful walnuts

Peel the onion and slice thinly. Wash the radishes and slice thinly. Mix the remaining ingredients in a saucepan with 100 ml of water and bring to the boil. Cook for 5 minutes over medium heat, stirring to dissolve the sugar. Place the onion and radish slices in an airtight jar, pour the brine and herbs into the jar and leave to cool at room temperature. Close the jar and set aside in the fridge for 24 hours before using.

Mix the cornflour with the coconut milk in a small saucepan. Add the yeast, brine, garlic and onion powders and salt and mix. Bring to the boil and simmer for 2 minutes, whisking constantly. When the sauce has thickened, remove the saucepan from the hob and leave to cool.

Cut the pear into slices. Heat a little oil in a frying pan and cook the pear slices for 2 minutes on each side until tender and slightly golden.

Peel and chop the garlic, then whiz, pulsing all the ingredients for the pesto until smooth but still slightly grainy.

Spread one side of the bread slices with margarine before placing them on a plate, buttered side down. Spread 2 slices of bread with pesto, add the roasted pear, cheese sauce, pickles and chopped walnuts. Close with the remaining 2 slices of bread, buttered side up.

Brown the sandwiches in a large non-stick frying pan over medium heat for 2–3 minutes on each side.

TIPS AND VARIATIONS
This cheese sauce can be made in minutes and is ideal for topping burgers or drizzling over nachos, pasta, pizza or Canadian poutine-style fries.

BURRITO WITH CREAMY PUMPKIN AND QUINOA

I thought I was very familiar with them, but I rediscovered burritos on my trip to Mexico. I particularly remember a burrito stuffed with red beans, avocado and nopal *(prickly pear cactus). In a nutshell, just local emblematic ingredients. That's what inspired this version of a quinoa and creamy pumpkin burrito.*

GLUTEN-FREE

**MAKES 2 LARGE BURRITOS
PREP TIME: 20 MINUTES
COOKING TIME: 30 MINUTES**

FOR THE CREAMY PUMPKIN
100 g pumpkin (whatever variety
 you like)
1 tbsp olive oil
1 pinch salt
½ garlic clove
40 g soy yoghurt
20 g tahini
1 tbsp lemon juice
1 tbsp soy sauce
1 tsp maple syrup
½ tsp paprika
¼ tsp salt

FOR THE QUINOA
120 g quinoa
8 large black olives
1 tbsp sesame seeds
1 tbsp lemon juice
1 tbsp soy sauce
½ tsp ground cumin
15 g pumpkin seeds
10 g sesame seeds
Zest ½ lemon
Salt and pepper

FOR THE BURRITOS
2 large maize or wheat tortillas
2 handfuls baby spinach leaves
1 small bunch fresh coriander,
 chopped

Preheat the oven to 200°C (gas mark 6) and line a baking tray with parchment paper. Peel the pumpkin and cut into cubes. Arrange the cubes on a baking tray, drizzle with oil, add a pinch of salt and toss to coat the pumpkin. Bake for 20 minutes, until the pumpkin is tender (check with the tip of a knife).

Peel and finely chop the garlic. Whiz the pumpkin, garlic and the remaining ingredients until smooth and silky. Taste and adjust the seasoning.

Tip the quinoa into a sieve and rinse under running water before tipping it into a saucepan with two parts water to one part quinoa. Bring to the boil, reduce the heat to low, cover and cook for 10–12 minutes, until tender.

Pit and chop the olives. Put the cooked quinoa into a bowl, add the olives and the remaining ingredients, season and mix.

Heat the tortillas in a microwave for a few minutes to soften. Place a tortilla flat on the worktop. Spread pumpkin purée over it, then add the quinoa, spinach leaves and chopped coriander. Fold the side closest to you over the tortilla and over the stuffing, then fold both vertical sides towards the centre, holding it firmly with your hands. Enjoy the burrito at room temperature or heat it in a non-stick frying pan or in the oven for a few minutes on each side.

TIPS AND VARIATIONS
Turn this dish into a burrito bowl by serving the quinoa and pumpkin purée with cooked and raw vegetables (tomato, red cabbage, broccoli, avocado, etc.), roasted chickpeas (see recipe p. 105) and homemade tortilla chips (see recipe p. 141).

BLT: THE FAMOUS AUBERGINE BACON, LETTUCE AND TOMATO SANDWICH

Behind this short, punchy and slightly intriguing name is a sandwich that's very popular in the United States, extremely simple, but packed with flavour. It consists of three ingredients: bacon, lettuce and tomato slices, which is where the three letters come from. You could say that BLT is to Americans what bangers and mash is to the British! But let's break with tradition with this veggie BLT with a filling of aubergine bacon and white bean hummus.

MAKES 2 SANDWICHES
PREP TIME: 20 MINUTES
COOKING TIME: 30 MINUTES

FOR THE AUBERGINE BACON
½ aubergine
2 tbsp olive oil
1 tbsp soy sauce
1 tbsp maple syrup
½ tsp smoked paprika
1 pinch salt

FOR THE BEAN HUMMUS
15 g pine nuts
150 g tinned white beans
½ onion
½ garlic clove
30 g tahini
2 tbsp olive oil
2 tbsp lemon juice
Salt and pepper

FOR THE SANDWICH
1 large tomato
4 gherkins
4 lettuce leaves
4 slices bread (sandwich or
  farmhouse)

Preheat the oven to 180°C (gas mark 4) and line a baking tray with parchment paper. Rinse, dry and cut the aubergine lengthwise into thin slices. Mix the remaining ingredients in a bowl and brush the aubergine slices with the marinade before arranging them on the baking tray. Place in the oven for 10 minutes, then brush the aubergine slices again with the marinade and cook for a further 5–7 minutes until they are nicely grilled. Leave to cool.

Roast the pine nuts at 170°C (gas mark 3–4) for 10–15 minutes, until golden. Keep a close eye on them to prevent burning. Leave to cool.

Rinse and drain the white beans. Peel and finely slice the onion and garlic. Whiz all the ingredients for the hummus until smooth and silky. Taste and adjust the seasoning.

Slice the tomato and gherkins. Wash the lettuce leaves. Spread the bread slices generously with hummus, place a lettuce leaf, tomato slices, gherkins and the aubergine bacon on top. Enjoy the BLTs immediately or wrap in cling film to eat them later in the day.

TIPS AND VARIATIONS
- You can swap the white bean hummus with chickpea hummus, tapenade, tomato caviar or broccoli guacamole (see recipe p. 141).
- Feel free to add the vegetables of your choice: carrot ribbons, cucumber slices, avocado, radish, raw beetroot ... or even slices of marinated tofu (see recipe p. 68).

MAINS

SOCCA, BEAN SALAD WITH FRESH HERBS AND A LEMONY TAHINI DRESSING

It's impossible not to offer you a recipe for socca, as I'm so fond of this culinary speciality from Nice. A thick chickpea flour flatbread, it's traditionally cooked in a large shallow copper pan. Served hot, in pieces cut straight from the pan, it's still prepared this way at markets and in specialised shops in the region of Nice. It's a real treat to eat on the go, as an appetiser, sitting on a bench or while going for a walk. At home, I like to prepare socca like a large flatbread, topped with a tahini cream and a fresh herb salad.

GLUTEN-FREE

SERVES 2
PREP TIME: 30 MINUTES
COOKING TIME: 10 MINUTES
**MARINATING TIME: 20
 MINUTES**
RESTING TIME: 15 MINUTES

**FOR THE BEAN AND
 COURGETTE SALAD**
120 g beans (fresh or frozen)
1 small courgette
1 garlic clove
30 g green olives, pitted
6 mint leaves
6 basil leaves
2 tbsp olive oil
2 tbsp lemon juice
2 tsp lemon zest
20 g pine nuts
Salt and pepper

FOR THE DRESSING
120 g natural non-dairy yoghurt
 (like Greek yoghurt)
40 g tahini
1 garlic clove
1 tbsp olive oil
1 tbsp lemon juice
1 tsp maple syrup
1 pinch salt

FOR THE SOCCA
200 g chickpea flour
½ tsp ground cumin
¼ tsp turmeric
¼ tsp salt
2 tbsp olive oil

PLUS
Mesclun salad leaves

Cook the beans for 10 minutes in a saucepan of boiling water or 5 minutes in a microwave with a little water. They should be al dente. Leave to cool for a few minutes, then peel the beans.

Use a potato peeler to cut the courgette into ribbons. Peel and finely chop the garlic. Slice the olives. Chop the mint and basil.

Mix the garlic, herbs, oil, lemon juice and zest, salt and pepper in a salad bowl to make the dressing. Add the beans, courgette ribbons, pine nuts and olives and toss gently. Leave to macerate for 20 minutes in the fridge.

Mix all the ingredients for the yoghurt cream in a bowl until smooth. Taste and adjust the seasoning. Set aside in the fridge.

Combine the chickpea flour, cumin, turmeric and salt in a bowl. Add the oil and 150 ml of water and mix until smooth and lump-free. Leave at room temperature for 15 minutes.

Heat a large, lightly oiled non-stick frying pan. Pour half of the batter into the frying pan and allow it to spread over the base of the pan. Cook for 2–3 minutes until small bubbles appear on the surface and it comes away easily from the bottom of the frying pan. Carefully turn the socca over and cook the other side for 2 minutes. Repeat the process with all the batter, oiling the frying pan as necessary.

Leave the soccas to cool for a few minutes before spreading a generous amount of yoghurt cream on them and serving with the salad and a handful of mesclun.

RATATOUILLE CHACHOUKA-STYLE WITH QUINOA

This is another traditional dish that's made a comeback. Chachouka (shakshuka, tchektchouka...) is a Maghrebi speciality of peppers, tomatoes, onions and chillies cooked in a cast-iron pan with eggs added at the end of cooking. This traditional, warm and sunny dish is reminiscent of our beloved Provençal ratatouille. Like a bridge between the two continents, this is my ratatouille with quinoa, chachouka-style.

GLUTEN-FREE

SERVES 4
PREP TIME: 10 MINUTES
COOKING TIME: 20 MINUTES

2 large tomatoes
1 red pepper
150 g courgettes
150 g aubergines
¼ onion
1 garlic clove
1 tbsp olive oil
5 sprigs fresh thyme
120 g quinoa
1 tsp dried oregano
1 tsp paprika
1 pinch Espelette pepper
50 g tomato paste
150 g cooked chickpeas
Salt and pepper

PLUS
Non-dairy ricotta
Fresh parsley, chopped
Slices of toasted bread or
 homemade socca (see recipe
 p. 90)

Dice the tomatoes. Seed the pepper and cut into strips. Dice the courgette and aubergine. Peel and chop the onion and garlic.

Heat the oil in a frying pan and gently fry the onion and garlic for 2 minutes over medium heat, stirring regularly. Add the tomatoes, pepper, courgette, aubergine and thyme and cook for 3 minutes.

Rinse and drain the quinoa before tipping it into the frying pan with the oregano, paprika, chilli, tomato paste and 250 ml of water. Stir, cover and simmer for 10 minutes until the quinoa is tender. If necessary, add a little water during cooking to keep the ratatouille moist. Add the drained chickpeas and cook for a further 3 minutes. Season to taste.

Serve the ratatouille hot or cold, topped with crumbled ricotta and chopped fresh parsley, accompanied by toasted bread.

TIPS AND VARIATIONS
- The great thing about ratatouille is that it can be made in advance and kept in the fridge for several days. Prepare a fair amount to accompany dishes throughout the week.
- It can be eaten hot or cold, on a slice of bread or with a rice salad. Use any leftovers to fill a pie or to make a crumble.

TOMATO AND GARDEN PEACH SALAD, FRESH ALMOND CHEESE

I started making this salad last summer in Montpellier, when my father's garden had just produced its very first crop of juicy, sweet, sun-kissed heirloom tomatoes! With a few peaches from the market, all you need is a little dressing, a handful of toasted seeds, nuts and a little crumbled non-dairy cheese to make the tastiest and most refreshing salad in a jiffy.

GLUTEN-FREE

SERVES 4
PREP TIME: 20 MINUTES
COOKING TIME: 5 MINUTES
SOAKING TIME: 8 HOURS
RESTING TIME: OVERNIGHT

FOR THE ALMOND CHEESE
140 g whole or blanched almonds
20 g nutritional yeast
2 tbsp lemon juice
1 tsp garlic powder
½ tsp salt

FOR THE CRISP
20 g pistachios
1 tbsp mustard seeds

FOR THE VINAIGRETTE
50 g raspberries
6 tbsp olive oil
3 tbsp balsamic vinegar
Salt and pepper

FOR THE SALAD
4 large heirloom tomatoes
6 peaches
Olive oil
Salt and pepper

Blanch the almonds for 5 minutes in a saucepan of boiling water if they are not already blanched. Drain the almonds before placing them in a bowl filled with water. Leave to soak for 8 hours at room temperature. Drain again and remove the skins.

Whiz the blanched almonds with the yeast, lemon juice, garlic powder, salt and 2–3 tablespoons of water to a smooth, slightly grainy consistency (add water gradually to get the right texture). Set the almond cheese aside in an airtight container in the fridge. It can be eaten immediately, but tastes even better the next day.

Crush the pistachios. Toast the pistachios and mustard seeds for a few minutes in a hot, dry frying pan, stirring regularly. Leave to cool.

Whiz all the ingredients for the vinaigrette until smooth. Taste and adjust the seasoning.

Wash the tomatoes and cut into segments or slices. Stone the peaches and cut into segments.

Arrange the tomatoes and peaches in a large dish. Drizzle with the vinaigrette, a drizzle of oil, and sprinkle with the toasted pistachios and mustard seeds. Season and crumble the almond cheese over the salad.

TIPS AND VARIATIONS
This fresh almond cheese has a silky texture and a mild taste that makes it the perfect accompaniment to many dishes. Crumble it over salads, roasted vegetables, pasta and stews. It's also delicious on toast, with a soup or salad.

BAKED AUBERGINE WITH YOGHURT SAUCE AND DUKKAH

Some dishes leave an indelible impression, like aubergines roasted over charcoal long enough for its charred skin to peel away, revealing its beautifully creamy flesh and a delicate smoky aroma. A flavour so intense that a touch of yoghurt and a hint of dukkah are enough to elevate it. If you don't have a barbecue, this oven-roasted aubergine works just as well.

GLUTEN-FREE

SERVES 2
PREP TIME: 20 MINUTES
COOKING TIME: 30 MINUTES

FOR THE ROASTED AUBERGINE
1 aubergine
1 tbsp olive oil
1 pinch salt

FOR THE PISTACHIO DUKKAH
20 g pistachios
10 g sesame seeds
1 tbsp coriander seeds
1 tbsp cumin seeds
½ tbsp fleur de sel
¼ tsp black peppercorns

**FOR THE YOGHURT AND
  TAHINI SAUCE**
150 g thick non-dairy yoghurt
 (Greek style)
20 g tahini
1 tbsp lemon juice
1 tsp maple syrup
¼ tsp ground cumin
¼ tsp ground cardamom
Salt and pepper

FOR DECORATION
Fresh parsley
Pomegranate seeds
Lemon zest
Green olives

Preheat the oven to 200°C (gas mark 6) and line a baking tray with parchment paper.

Cut the aubergine in half lengthwise without peeling it. Use the tip of a knife to score the flesh about 4 mm deep, taking care not to pierce the skin. Arrange the aubergine halves on a baking tray, skin side down, drizzle with olive oil and season with salt. Bake for 30 minutes or until very soft. Check for doneness by pricking them with the tip of a knife. Adjust the cooking time according to the size of the aubergine.

Heat a dry frying pan over high heat to toast the pistachios for 2–3 minutes, stirring regularly. Remove the pistachios from the pan. Do the same with the sesame seeds, toasting them for 1 minute while stirring to prevent them from burning. Toast the coriander and cumin seeds for 1 minute.

Coarsely pound the pistachios, sesame seeds, coriander seeds, cumin seeds and pepper with a mortar and pestle. Add the fleur de sel at the end.

Prepare the sauce by mixing all the ingredients in a bowl. Taste and adjust the seasoning.

Serve the roasted aubergine warm on a bed of sauce, garnished with chopped fresh parsley, pomegranate seeds, lemon zest, sliced green olives, and sprinkled with dukkah.

TIPS AND VARIATIONS
- Dukkah can be stored for months in a cool dry airtight container at room temperature. Prepare a jar of it to sprinkle over dishes, salads, sandwiches and even to add to your baked goods such as naan dough (see recipe p. 73).
- Traditionally, dukkah is made with hazelnuts. You can swap the pistachios for almonds, and add walnuts, sunflower or pumpkin seeds.

MUSHROOM AND LEEK RISOTTO WITH PRALINE-COFFEE DRESSING

When it comes to good things, the Italians don't mess around. Risotto is popular all over the world, but in its country of origin it's a highly respected dish. And for good reason; this flavoursome comforting dish, simple in appearance, requires a very precise technique that the Italians have mastered over the years. I love this recipe because it can be adapted in a thousand ways and allows you to take full advantage of each season's produce.

GLUTEN-FREE

SERVES 2
PREP TIME: 15 MINUTES
COOKING TIME: 25 MINUTES

FOR THE RISOTTO
1 litre vegetable stock
100 g white mushrooms
½ yellow onion
½ garlic clove
1 tbsp vegan margarine
2 tbsp olive oil
1 tsp dried thyme
1 tsp dried sage
200 g arborio rice (special rice
  for risotto)
40 ml dry white wine
1 leek
50 g non-dairy cream
¼ tsp ground nutmeg
2 handfuls rocket leaves
1 handful roasted hazelnuts
Salt and pepper

FOR THE VINAIGRETTE
2 tbsp espresso coffee
1 tbsp hazelnut butter
1 tbsp cider vinegar
1 tbsp maple syrup
1 tsp mustard
Salt and pepper

Bring the vegetable stock to the boil in a large saucepan, then reduce the heat to very low. It needs to be hot while you make the risotto.

Wash and finely slice the mushrooms. Peel and finely chop the onion and garlic.

Melt the margarine in a high-sided frying pan with 1 tablespoon of olive oil. Add the garlic, onion, thyme and sage and fry for 3 minutes over medium heat without browning. Tip in the rice, toss to coat and fry for 2 minutes until translucent. Pour in the white wine. When the alcohol has evaporated, pour the first ladleful of stock into the pan and stir regularly. It should remain at a simmer. When the stock has almost been totally absorbed, pour in another ladleful. Repeat until the stock has been used up and the rice is cooked through (about 25 minutes). Add the mushrooms after 20 minutes of cooking.

Split and wash the leek. Keep only the white part. Cook the white part of the leek in a saucepan of boiling water for 6 minutes. Drain and fry in a frying pan with 1 tablespoon of oil for 3 minutes, turning regularly to brown it all over. Remove the saucepan from the hob, add salt and cut the leek into chunks.

Prepare the vinaigrette by mixing all the ingredients in a bowl. Taste and adjust the seasoning if necessary.

When the rice is tender, add the cream, nutmeg and season to taste. Serve the risotto hot on a bed of rocket leaves. Top with chunks of leek and roasted chopped hazelnuts, and drizzle with the vinaigrette.

TIPS AND VARIATIONS
In autumn and winter, serve the risotto with diced roasted pumpkin and parsnips, sautéed chanterelles, chestnuts and walnuts. In spring, it's delicious with green asparagus and petit pois. In summer, enjoy this risotto with courgette, aubergine and bell pepper.

SILKY MAC AND CHEESE WITH CREAMED VEGETABLES

One of my most special memories is the pasta au gratin my mother used to make: pasta and grated cheese, topped with crumbled rusks for crunchiness. How can such a simple dish be so good? Because it combines everything needed for a successful recipe: basic ingredients, deliciousness and a lot of love. A memory I've immortalised with my own version of mac and cheese.

GLUTEN-FREE OPTION

SERVES 4
PREP TIME: 20 MINUTES
SOAKING TIME: 20 MINUTES
COOKING TIME: 35 MINUTES

FOR THE GRATIN
50 g cashew nuts
250 g potatoes
120 g carrots
300 g pasta (macaroni or rigatoni, gluten-free if necessary)
1 yellow onion
1 garlic clove
30 g nutritional yeast
20 g mustard
180 ml plain almond milk
2 tbsp cider vinegar
½ tsp smoked paprika
Salt and pepper

FOR THE TOPPING
30 g sunflower seeds
50 g ground almonds
1 tbsp nutritional yeast
½ tsp garlic powder
¼ tsp salt
1½ tbsp coconut oil
1 tbsp olive oil

Soak the cashew nuts in hot water for 20 minutes. Rinse and drain.

Peel the potatoes and carrots and cut into medium-sized cubes. Cook the vegetables in a large saucepan of boiling water for 15–20 minutes until tender. Drain and set aside.

Cook the pasta in boiling water according to the instructions on the packet but reduce the cooking time by 2 minutes. Drain the pasta and keep it hot.

Peel and finely chop the onion and garlic. Gently fry in a frying pan with a little water or 1 tablespoon of olive oil for 2 minutes until translucent.

Preheat the oven to 180°C (gas mark 4). Put the cooked carrots and potatoes, onion, garlic, cashew nuts, yeast, mustard, almond milk, vinegar and paprika into the jar of a blender, season and whiz to a smooth, creamy sauce. If the sauce is too thick, add a little almond milk until you achieve the right consistency.

Chop the sunflower seeds. Mix the ground almonds, sunflower seeds, yeast, garlic and salt in a bowl. Add the coconut oil and olive oil and mix to a slightly dry and crumbly texture.

Tip the pasta into the gratin dish. Pour the sauce over it and toss to coat well. Sprinkle with topping and bake for 15 minutes, until the topping begins to brown. Leave to cool for a few minutes before serving hot.

TIPS AND VARIATIONS
The mac and cheese sauce can be stored for up to 5 days in an airtight container in the fridge. Make a larger quantity and use for pasta dishes, Mexican recipes (tacos, burritos, quesadillas, nachos), burgers, sandwiches, to go with chips, or simply as a dip served with crudités or tortilla chips.

SPAGHETTI CACIO E PEPE WITH NON-DAIRY PARMESAN

Sometimes the simplest things are the best. And *pasta cacio e pepe* (literally 'pasta with cheese and pepper') is proof of this! In Italy, this speciality is made using a specific variety of sheep's milk cheese from the region of Rome. Although the Italians might disapprove, here's a completely plant-based version that's just as delicious topped with Parmesan-style tuiles.

GLUTEN-FREE OPTION

SERVES 2
PREP TIME: 20 MINUTES
COOKING TIME: 30 MINUTES

**FOR THE NON-DAIRY
 PARMESAN**
15 g rice flour (white or
 wholegrain)
15 g ground almonds
10 g nutritional yeast
1 tsp dried oregano
¼ tsp salt
4 tsp olive oil
1 garlic clove
15 g pine nuts

FOR THE SPAGHETTI
60 g cashew nuts
200 g spaghetti (gluten-free if
 necessary)
60 ml plain almond milk
20 g nutritional yeast
15 g white miso
1 tbsp gherkin brine (or white
 wine vinegar)
1 pinch salt
1 tbsp olive oil
1 tsp black pepper, preferably
 freshly ground

Preheat the oven to 170°C (gas mark 3-4).

Mix the ingredients for the non-dairy parmesan in a bowl until you have a grainy, slightly crumbly mixture. If it's too dry, add a little olive oil. Spread the paste between two sheets of parchment paper to make an even layer about 3 mm thick. Place on a baking tray and bake for 10 minutes. Leave to cool on a wire rack. Don't touch the tuile until it's completely cool!

Roast the cashew nuts in the oven at 180°C (gas mark 4) for 10 minutes (this step is optional but helps brings out the flavours).

Cook the spaghetti in a saucepan of boiling water for 2 minutes less than the time recommended on the packet. Drain over a bowl to save the cooking water for the sauce.

Put the cashew nuts, almond milk, yeast, miso, brine, salt and 100 ml of the pasta water into a blender. Whiz to a smooth cream. Adjust the amount of water until you have the right consistency.

Heat the oil in a large frying pan. Add the pepper and fry for 1 minute, stirring regularly. Pour in the sauce. When it starts to bubble, add the spaghetti and toss to coat. Cook for 2 minutes, adding a little of the cooking water if necessary.

Serve immediately after sprinkling the dish with the crumbled non-dairy parmesan.

TIPS AND VARIATIONS
- Preferably use black peppercorns and pound with a mortar and pestle or grind at the last moment to ensure freshness and aroma.
- Non-dairy parmesan is ideal for enhancing your pasta dishes, risottos, grilled vegetables and salads. Prepare a larger quantity and store in a glass jar in a dry place.

Caesar-Style Kale and Crunchy Chickpea Granola Salad

No, the Caesar salad was not invented by the famous Roman general, but by an Italian-American chef called Caesar Cardini at his Mexican restaurant. It quickly became the most popular salad in the United States. Originally consisting of lettuce, garlic croutons, the dressing, parmesan cheese and eggs, other ingredients, such as avocado and tomato, were added over time. Why not innovate with this version made with kale and crispy chickpea granola?

GLUTEN-FREE

SERVES 4
PREP TIME: 20 MINUTES
COOKING TIME: 35 MINUTES
RESTING TIME: 1 HOUR

FOR THE CHICKPEA GRANOLA
160 g tinned chickpeas (you'll
  need the liquid)
2 tbsp coconut oil
30 g cashew nuts
30 g pumpkin seeds
20 g walnuts
20 g pine nuts
4 sprigs thyme
1 tbsp salted soy sauce
1 tbsp maple syrup
Zest ½ lemon
¼ tsp salt
15 g aquafaba

FOR THE CAESAR SAUCE
80 g thick non-dairy yoghurt
80 g tahini
20 g capers
1 garlic clove
4 tbsp lemon juice
4 tbsp olive oil
4 tbsp mustard
1 tbsp maple syrup
Salt and pepper

FOR THE KALE SALAD
8 large kale leaves
8 salad leaves
2 avocados

Preheat the oven to 180°C (gas mark 4) and line a baking tray with parchment paper. Drain and rinse the chickpeas, keeping a little of the aquafaba water for the rest of the recipe. Dry the chickpeas with kitchen paper or a tea towel and skin them. Arrange the chickpeas on the baking tray and drizzle with the melted coconut oil. Stir to coat well. Bake for 20 minutes, until golden and crispy. Leave to cool for a few minutes.

Lower the oven temperature to 160°C (gas mark 3).

Place the roasted chickpeas, cashew nuts, pumpkin seeds, walnuts, pine nuts and chopped thyme in a bowl. Add the soy sauce, maple syrup, lemon zest, salt and mix. Pour 15 g of aquafaba into a bowl and whisk by hand or with an electric whisk until frothy. Add the frothy aquafaba to the mixture and mix gently to coat all the ingredients. Spread the mixture on the baking tray in an even layer that's not too thick. Bake for 15 minutes until the granola is nice and golden. Leave to cool for at least 1 hour.

Whiz all the ingredients for the Caesar sauce with 3–4 tablespoons of water until it is creamy. Add water gradually until you have the right consistency. Taste and adjust the seasoning.

Wash the kale and salad leaves and chop coarsely. Arrange the lettuce and kale in a salad bowl, pour half the dressing over them and mix.

Scoop the flesh from the avocados and dice. Serve the salad with the Caesar sauce and diced avocado, sprinkled with the granola.

TIPS AND VARIATIONS
- Feel free to add other vegetables to your Caesar salad: cherry tomatoes, radishes, carrot ribbons, cucumbers, etc.
- Sprinkle the salad with crumbled non-dairy parmesan for an even more authentic experience (see recipe for *spaghetti cacio e pepe*, p. 102).

BREADED CAULIFLOWER, POLENTA FRIES AND PETIT POIS MAYONNAISE: MY VERSION OF FISH AND CHIPS

The Americans have their burgers, the Brits have fish and chips. Fish fried in beer batter, crispy chips, a pinch of salt and a splash of malt vinegar — that's all it takes to make this simple, satisfying dish that's the hallmark of British fast food! And it's still very popular throughout Britain today. Whether in city centres or small coastal harbours, people rush to order fish and chips as a takeaway for food on the go. Here, there are no fish or potatoes, but a breaded cauliflower steak and crispy polenta fries.

GLUTEN-FREE OPTION

SERVES 2
PREP TIME: 40 MINUTES
COOKING TIME: 1 HOUR 20 MINUTES
RESTING TIME: 30 MINUTES

FOR THE BREADED CAULIFLOWER
1 small cauliflower
60 g plain soy yoghurt
20 ml almond milk
50 g chickpea flour
2 tbsp nutritional yeast
1 tbsp lemon juice
1 tsp maple syrup
¼ tsp kala namak salt
¼ tsp ground pepper
½ sheet nori seaweed
30 g breadcrumbs
20 g panko breadcrumbs
Olive oil

FOR THE POLENTA FRIES
50 g chickpea flour
50 g polenta
1 tbsp olive oil
½ tsp ground turmeric
¼ tsp salt

FOR THE KALE CHIPS
2 large kale leaves
1 tbsp olive oil
1 tbsp nutritional yeast
½ tsp garlic powder
1 pinch salt

FOR THE PETIT POIS MAYONNAISE
100 g cooked petits pois
40 g soy yoghurt
1 garlic clove
2 tbsp olive oil
2 tbsp lemon juice
1 tbsp maple syrup
1 tsp wasabi (or hot mustard)
Salt and pepper

Preheat the oven to 200°C (gas mark 6) and line a baking tray with parchment paper.

Cut two slices about 2 cm thick from the middle section of the cauliflower. Steam or cook the cauliflower slices in a frying pan with a little water for 5 minutes to soften.

Whiz the yoghurt, milk, chickpea flour, yeast, lemon juice, maple syrup, salt, pepper and crumbled nori seaweed to a batter. Transfer the mixture to a dish. Combine the breadcrumbs and the panko breadcrumbs in a plate.

Place the cauliflower slices one by one in the batter and coat both sides completely before dipping in the breadcrumbs. Handle them with care as they are quite fragile. Place the cauliflower slices on the baking tray and drizzle with oil. Bake for 15 minutes, then turn the slices over and bake for a further 10–15 minutes, until the breadcrumbs are golden brown. Keep it hot.

Mix the chickpea flour and polenta in a bowl. Heat the oil with 350 ml of water, turmeric and salt in a saucepan. When the water starts to boil, tip in the flour and polenta mixture, whisking to combine. Reduce the heat to low and cook for 2–3 minutes, stirring constantly, until thickened. Pour the mixture into a dish lined with parchment paper in an even layer and leave to cool for 30 minutes. Carefully turn out the hardened polenta before cutting it into sticks. Arrange the fries on a baking tray lined with parchment paper, brush with oil and sprinkle with a pinch of salt. Place in the oven for 25 minutes, turning the fries halfway through baking so that they are golden brown all over.

Lower the oven temperature to 160°C (gas mark 3).

Rinse and dry the kale leaves before cutting into pieces. Place the pieces in a bowl, add the oil, yeast, garlic powder and salt and toss. Arrange the kale on a baking tray lined with parchment paper and bake for 20–25 minutes, until crisp. Keep a close eye on them to avoid them burning.

Peel and chop the garlic, then whiz all the mayonnaise ingredients until smooth. If it's too thick, add a little water.

Serve the breaded cauliflower with the fries, kale chips and petit pois mayonnaise.

TIPS AND VARIATIONS
For a gluten-free version, swap all the breadcrumbs for gluten-free breadcrumbs.

CREAMY AND CRISPY QUICHE LORRAINE WITH FILO PASTRY

How can we talk about traditional French cuisine without mentioning one of the most emblematic recipes in France? My nomination is quiche Lorraine! But on my trip to Istanbul, I discovered myriad possibilities that filo pastry can offer: it's used to make their famous baklava, but also many other desserts, pastries and savoury pies. This is what inspired me to create this version of quiche Lorraine with smoked tofu, where the silkiness of the cream meets the unbeatable crispness of the filo pastry.

SERVES 6
PREP TIME: 30 MINUTES
COOKING TIME: 40 MINUTES
RESTING TIME: 1 HOUR

FOR DECORATION
125 g smoked (or plain) firm tofu
2 tbsp soy sauce
1 tbsp maple syrup
1 tbsp tomato paste
1 tbsp olive oil
½ tsp smoked paprika
½ yellow onion
1 tbsp olive oil
Salt and pepper

FOR THE FILLING
300 g silken tofu
150 g soy cream
20 g chickpea flour
1 tbsp mustard
3 tbsp nutritional yeast
1 tsp garlic powder
1 tsp onion powder
1 pinch ground nutmeg
¼ tsp pepper
¼ tsp black salt

FOR THE CRISPY PASTRY
5 sheets filo pastry
Olive oil

Preheat the oven to 180°C (gas mark 4). Oil a high rimmed mould about 24 cm in diameter.

Cut the tofu into matchsticks. Mix the soy sauce, maple syrup, tomato paste, olive oil and paprika in a bowl. Add the tofu and stir. Gently fry the tofu in a frying pan for 5 minutes, stirring regularly, until slightly caramelised. Season to taste.

Peel and thinly slice the onion. Heat the oil in a frying pan and gently fry the onion for 3 minutes until lightly browned.

Place all the ingredients for the quiche filling in a blender and whiz until smooth and evenly textured. Add the onion and the tofu.

Brush a sheet of filo pastry generously with oil before placing it in the oiled mould. Repeat with another sheet, placing it across the first one in a different direction. Repeat with the remaining sheets. Cut off the overhanging filo and slightly crumple the edges. Pour the quiche filling into the filo pastry shell and spread it evenly. Bake for 30 minutes, until the centre of the quiche is fairly firm and the edges of the pastry are golden and crisp.

Leave to cool for 1 hour at room temperature for the quiche to firm up nicely before cutting into slices.

TIPS AND VARIATIONS
- Filo pastry adds a crispness that balances beautifully with the creaminess of the quiche. Large sheets are sold in oriental grocery shops and supermarkets. You can also use classic puff pastry or shortcrust pastry to make this recipe.
- Filo pastry sheets dry quickly when they come into contact with air. Don't take them out of the packet until the last moment and then keep them under a slightly damp tea towel while you assemble the base.

PALAK PANEER: CREAMY SPINACH AND CHICKPEA CURRY

A far cry from canteen creamed spinach, *palak paneer* is a creamy, spicy curry that is emblematic of Indian cuisine. It's made with cooked whizzed spinach *(palak)* and *paneer*, an Indian fresh cheese. Here, chickpeas replace the cheese, but the taste is just as delicious.

GLUTEN-FREE

**SERVES 2 AS A MAIN COURSE
 OR 4 AS A SIDE DISH
PREP TIME: 10 MINUTES
COOKING TIME: 15 MINUTES**

1 yellow onion
2 cloves garlic
1 cm fresh ginger
1 cm lemongrass
2 tomatoes
1 tbsp coconut oil
1 tsp garam masala
½ tsp fenugreek (optional)
300 g fresh spinach
100 ml coconut milk
5 sprigs fresh coriander
100 g cooked chickpeas
1 coconut yoghurt
Salt and pepper

Peel and finely chop the onion and garlic. Finely chop the ginger and lemongrass. Dice the tomatoes.

Heat the coconut oil in a large frying pan. Add the onion, garlic, ginger and lemongrass and gently fry for 2 minutes without browning. Add the garam masala and fenugreek. Season and fry for 1 minute. Add the tomatoes and a little water and simmer for about 6 minutes, until the tomatoes are soft and the mixture has reduced. Lastly, add the spinach and coconut milk and leave the spinach to wilt for 2 minutes.

Pour the mixture into a blender, add the coriander and whiz to a smooth cream. Pour the mixture into a frying pan, add the rinsed and drained chickpeas and cook for 2 minutes over low heat.

Serve the palak paneer hot or warm with 1 spoonful of coconut yoghurt, chopped coriander and a pinch of cracked black pepper. Serve with naan (see recipe p. 73).

TIPS AND VARIATIONS

- Serve palak paneer as a main course with basmati rice, red lentil dahl (see recipe p. 116) and grilled diced tempeh, or as a starter or appetiser with homemade naan (see recipe p. 73).
- Whizzing the mixture gives a creamy, smooth texture that's ideal as a dip served with pita or crackers as an appetiser. Alternatively, you can leave the spinach whole and serve it as a main course with rice.
- Garam masala is a mixture of spices from India and widely used in Indian cuisine, but also in Réunionnais cooking. It can contain, among other things, caloupilé (curry leaves), coriander, cumin, nutmeg, cinnamon, cardamom, pepper and cloves. The ingredients in garam masala varies slightly from country to country. Although it's readily available in shops, you can make your own garam masala by toasting and then crushing 2 tablespoons of cumin seeds, 3 tablespoons of coriander seeds, 1 tablespoon of cardamom seeds, 1 teaspoon of black peppercorns, 1 teaspoon of cloves, ½ teaspoon of nutmeg, and 1 stick of cinnamon (or 1 teaspoon of ground cinnamon).

RICE PILAF WITH SPICES AND DRIED FRUIT

If there's one ingredient that symbolises traditional cuisine, it's rice. It's hardly a surprise as it's the world's number one staple food and features in many traditional recipes. Rice pilaf is definitely my favourite! 'Pilaf' refers to the cooking method in which the rice is first heated in oil and then cooked. The result is a soft, tender, delicious and extremely flavoursome rice. Here's a very simple and quick recipe with spices and dried fruit.

GLUTEN-FREE

SERVES 4
PREP TIME: 10 MINUTES
COOKING TIME: 20 MINUTES

200 g basmati rice
1 yellow onion
1 garlic clove
3 dried apricots
2 tbsp coconut oil
1 cinnamon stick
2 star anise
2 cardamom pods
2 bay leaves
15 g almonds
15 g pistachios
¼ tsp salt
¼ tsp pepper
20 g raisins
1 small bunch fresh parsley,
  chopped

Rinse the rice several times in cold water before draining it. Peel and finely chop the onion and garlic. Cut the dried apricots into small pieces.

Heat the coconut oil in a frying pan or saucepan. Add the onion and fry for 2 minutes over medium heat, without browning. Add the garlic, cinnamon, star anise and cardamom and fry for 2 minutes. Stir in the rice, bay leaves, almonds and pistachios, salt and pepper and gently fry for 2 minutes, stirring regularly.

Add 400 ml of water and then the apricots and raisins. Bring to the boil, then reduce the heat to low. Cover and cook for 10 minutes, stirring occasionally, until the rice is tender and all the water has been absorbed. Remove the saucepan from the hob and leave for 5 minutes without removing the lid.

Mix in the chopped parsley and serve hot.

TIPS AND VARIATIONS
- Serve rice pilaf as a main course with stir-fried vegetables, curry, palak paneer or red lentil dahl (see recipe p. 116).
- This recipe can be adapted endlessly by simply changing the seasoning. Here are some suggestions:
    - spices: cumin seeds, coriander seeds, mustard seeds, cloves, cardamom pods, etc.
    - nuts and seeds: walnuts, pecans, hazelnuts, cashew nuts, peanuts, pumpkin seeds, etc.
    - dried fruit: figs, dates, prunes, cranberries, goji berries, cape gooseberries, etc.

RED LENTIL DAHL, SAUTÉED RICE AND CUCUMBER SALAD

Dahl is an Indian dish made with pulses. The most famous one is *masoor dahl*; creamy and spicy it's made with red lentils. As with curries, there are many versions of dahl. This is my mother's recipe, ultra-creamy and with grated carrots that I serve with rice sautéed with coconut, peanuts and goji berries.

GLUTEN-FREE

SERVES 2
PREP TIME: 30 MINUTES
MARINATING TIME: 1 HOUR
COOKING TIME: 35 MINUTES

FOR THE CUCUMBER SALAD
80 g cucumber
2 tbsp rice wine vinegar
1 tbsp soy sauce
1 tsp sesame oil
1 tsp maple syrup
1 tbsp seaweed flakes

FOR THE DAHL
¼ yellow onion
½ garlic clove
30 g carrots
1 tbsp coconut oil
½ tsp fresh ginger, grated (or ground)
1 tbsp desiccated coconut
½ tsp turmeric
½ tsp ground coriander
½ tsp paprika
50 g dried red lentils
30 ml coconut milk
1 tbsp tomato paste
1 tbsp soy sauce
1 pinch salt
1 small bunch coriander

FOR THE SAUTÉED RICE
100 g basmati rice
1 cm fresh ginger
½ stick lemongrass
1 tbsp coconut oil
1 tsp coriander seeds
1 tsp sesame seeds
10 g peanuts
10 g desiccated coconut
10 g goji berries
Salt and pepper

Use a mandoline to slice the cucumber thinly. Mix the rice vinegar, soy sauce, sesame oil and maple syrup in a bowl. Add the cucumber slices and the seaweed, mix and set aside in the fridge for 1 hour.

Peel and chop the onion and garlic. Peel and finely grate the carrot.

Heat the oil in a saucepan and gently fry the onion over medium heat for 2 minutes, stirring regularly until slightly browned. Add the garlic, ginger, coconut, turmeric, coriander and paprika. Stir and gently fry for 2 minutes to infuse the flavours. Add the lentils, coconut milk, tomato paste, soy sauce, grated carrot, salt and 180 ml of water. Stir, bring to the boil and then simmer over medium heat for 15–20 minutes, until the liquid has been absorbed and the mixture thickens. Make sure there's always enough water during cooking. The dahl should be creamy. Keep it hot.

Cook the rice in 200 ml of water for 10 minutes, then drain. Peel and grate the ginger. Finely chop the lemongrass.

Heat the coconut oil in a frying pan and gently fry the ginger, lemongrass and coriander seeds for 2 minutes over medium heat. Add the sesame seeds, peanuts and coconut and gently fry for 2 minutes, stirring regularly and keeping an eye on the coconut so that it doesn't burn. Add the rice and goji berries, season with salt and gently fry for 2 minutes, stirring regularly.

Serve the hot dahl with the sautéed rice and cucumber salad, garnished with chopped coriander.

TIPS AND VARIATIONS
- Enjoy this dahl as a main course with sautéed vegetables and homemade naan (see recipe p. 73).
- You can swap the red lentils for green lentils or split peas.

Yellow Vegetable curry with pineapple and rice crackers

Originally, the word 'curry' referred to a mixture of spices that varied according to the cultural tradition of a country or even a region: coriander, cumin, turmeric, chilli, ginger, pepper, fennel, mustard ... and so on. Now, the term 'curry' is more widely used to refer to a dish prepared in a spicy sauce. In Réunion, the local version of curry is called Indian curry. I grew up with this delicious and flavoursome dish, and it's become a mainstay of my cooking.

GLUTEN-FREE

SERVES 2
PREP TIME: 20 MINUTES
COOKING TIME: 25 MINUTES

FOR THE CURRY
150 g sweet potato
130 g cauliflower
60 g fresh pineapple
¼ yellow onion
½ garlic clove
1 tsp coconut (or olive) oil
1 tsp curry powder
½ tsp turmeric
½ tsp chopped fresh ginger (or ground)
120 ml coconut milk
2 tbsp soy sauce
80 g cooked chickpeas
30 g cashew nuts
1 pinch salt

FOR THE RICE CRACKERS
2 sheets rice paper
Oil for frying

Wash and dice the sweet potato (keep the skin on if it's organic). Cut the cauliflower into florets. Dice the pineapple. Peel and chop the onion and garlic.

Heat the oil in a saucepan and gently fry the onion for 2 minutes over medium heat until lightly browned. Add the garlic, curry powder, turmeric and ginger and gently fry for 2 minutes. Add the sweet potato and gently fry for 2 minutes. Lastly, add the cauliflower, pineapple, coconut milk, soy sauce and 80 ml of water. Stir, bring to the boil, then simmer over medium heat for 10–15 minutes, until the sweet potato is tender. If the mixture is too dry, add a little water during cooking. The curry should be creamy and silky.

Add the chickpeas and cook for another 2 minutes. At the end of the cooking time, add the cashew nuts, season with salt and keep the curry hot.

Cut discs out of the rice sheets. Heat a little oil in a frying pan. When the temperature reaches 180°C and you see small 'veins' in the bottom of the pan, use tongs to submerge a disc of rice paper completely into the hot oil. It will swell up at once. Immediately remove the cracker from the oil and drain on kitchen paper. Repeat the process with the remaining discs of rice paper.

Serve the curry hot with the crackers.

TIPS AND VARIATIONS
- You can also serve the curry with rice, grains or homemade naan (see recipe p. 73).
- This recipe can be adapted to the seasonal vegetables available. You can use potatoes, broccoli, carrots, petit pois, green beans, turnips, courgettes, tomatoes, etc.

MY VERSION OF RÉUNION'S ROUGAIL SAUSAGE

Rougail sausages are part of my childhood. My mother, who is from Réunion, used to cook them for every special occasion. And she took it very seriously. You had to have the right ingredients, make sure they were fresh and of good quality, and above all prepare them with love, allowing the ingredients to simmer to release their aromas. Of course, nothing can match my mother's rougail, but this plant-based version has everything to delight your taste buds.

GLUTEN-FREE

SERVES 4
PREP TIME: 30 MINUTES
COOKING TIME: 20 MINUTES
SOAKING TIME: 20 MINUTES
RESTING TIME: 10 MINUTES

FOR THE SOY MEDALLIONS
150 g dried soy protein
500 ml vegetable stock
2 shallots
2 cloves garlic
2 tbsp soy sauce
2 tbsp mustard
2 tbsp nutritional yeast
1 tsp fennel seeds
1 tsp garlic powder
1 tsp ground oregano
3 sprigs fresh thyme
¼ tsp salt
¼ tsp pepper
40 g chickpea flour
2 tbsp olive oil

FOR THE ROUGAIL
4 tomatoes
2 yellow onions
2 cloves garlic
1 cm fresh ginger
2 small red chillies
1 tbsp olive oil
2 sprigs fresh thyme
1 tsp turmeric
Salt and pepper

PLUS
240 g basmati rice

Soak the soy protein in the hot vegetable stock for 20 minutes and then drain.

Peel and chop the shallots and garlic. Mix the soy protein, shallots, garlic, soy sauce, mustard, yeast, fennel seeds, garlic powder, oregano, thyme, salt and pepper to a thick paste. Tip the mixture into a bowl and stir in the chickpea flour. The resulting mixture should be firm enough to be worked by hand without sticking or falling apart. If it's too sticky, add a little flour. Cover and leave to rest in the fridge for 10 minutes.

Cook the rice in 450 ml of water until tender.

Take 1 tablespoon of mixture, shape it into a ball and then flatten into a thick medallion. Repeat with the remaining mixture. Heat the oil in a frying pan and cook the medallions for 4 minutes on each side. Leave to cool.

Dice the tomatoes. Peel and finely chop the onions and garlic. Peel and finely chop the ginger and chillies.

Gently fry the onions in a frying pan in the oil for 2 minutes over medium heat, without browning. Add the garlic, ginger, chillies and thyme and gently fry for 1 minute. Add the tomatoes and turmeric. Season and cook for 10 minutes over medium heat until the tomatoes are soft. If necessary, add a little water to prevent the mixture from drying out and catching on the bottom of the frying pan. Add the medallions and leave to simmer for 5 minutes.

Serve the rougail hot with the rice.

TIPS AND VARIATIONS
In a hurry? Swap the soy medallions for diced tempeh, tofu, chickpeas, beans or simply seasonal vegetables.

SPRING BOWL WITH RICE VERMICELLI, CRISPY VEGETABLES AND GRILLED TEMPEH

As good as spring rolls, but without the hassle of rolling them up! This colourful bowl filled with crunchy vegetables, diced marinated tempeh, rice vermicelli and a peanut sauce is like fireworks of flavour! Very fresh, nutritious and quick to prepare, it's perfect for a tasty summer lunch.

GLUTEN-FREE

MAKES 2 BOWLS
PREP TIME: 15 MINUTES
COOKING TIME: 10 MINUTES

FOR THE GRILLED TEMPEH
160 g plain tempeh
1 tbsp sesame oil
1 tbsp soy sauce
2 tsp maple syrup
2 tbsp tomato paste

FOR THE PEANUT SAUCE
60 g peanut butter
2 tbsp soy sauce
2 tsp maple syrup
2 tsp lime juice
1 tbsp rice vinegar
½ tsp ground ginger

FOR THE VERMICELLI
100 g rice vermicelli
1 tbsp sesame oil
1 tbsp soy sauce
1 tbsp rice vinegar

FOR DECORATION
¼ red cabbage
1 carrot
¼ cucumber
½ red pepper
40 g broad beans (or edamame)
4 sprigs fresh mint
4 sprigs fresh coriander
2 handfuls roasted peanuts

Dice the tempeh. Heat the oil in a frying pan and gently fry for 4 minutes over medium heat, stirring to brown all over. Add the soy sauce, maple syrup, tomato paste and 2 teaspoons of water. Cook for 1 minute, stirring constantly.

Mix all the ingredients for the sauce in a bowl with 2 tablespoons of water. Adjust the amount of water until you have the right consistency. If the sauce is too thick, add 1 spoonful of water at a time to thin it out.

Soak the vermicelli in a bowl of boiling water for 5 minutes until soft. Drain and mix the vermicelli with the oil, soy sauce and vinegar.

Finely chop the red cabbage. Peel the carrot and create fine ribbons using a vegetable peeler. Cut the cucumber into sticks. Remove the seeds from the pepper and cut into strips. Peel the beans.

Divide the rice vermicelli and raw vegetables between two large bowls. Add the grilled tempeh, mint and coriander. Top with the sauce and sprinkle the dish with crushed roasted peanuts.

TIPS AND VARIATIONS
- Tempeh is usually found in the fresh section of organic shops or Asian grocery shops. You can swap it for diced firm tofu or roasted chickpeas.
- Instead of rice vermicelli, swap them for any type of pasta (wheat noodles, rice noodles, soba noodles, konjac noodles, spaghetti, etc.), white rice or quinoa.
- This delicious flavoursome peanut sauce is perfect for seasoning all your Asian-influenced dishes, but also as a dip for egg rolls, samosas or spring rolls.

MIE GORENG WITH TEMPEH AND SAUTÉED VEGETABLES

Fried noodles are traditional in Asian cuisine. Each country and region has its own version. Japan has *yakisoba*, China *chow mein*, Thailand *pad thai* and Indonesia *mie goreng*. I first came across this very popular dish in Bali, where it's served in all *warungs* (small traditional restaurants) and by street vendors. It's a very simple but flavourful combination of noodles and stir-fried vegetables, seasoned with a sweet and sour sauce that adds a delicious caramelised taste to the dish.

GLUTEN-FREE OPTION

SERVES 2
PREP TIME: 10 MINUTES
COOKING TIME: 10 MINUTES

150 g wheat or rice noodles
150 g tempeh
½ red pepper
1 carrot
50 g broccoli
1 spring onion
1 small green chilli (optional)
1 shallot
1 garlic clove
1 cm fresh ginger
4 tbsp soy sauce
3 tbsp rice vinegar
1 tbsp maple syrup
1 tbsp sesame oil
50 g cooked and drained
  sweetcorn
30 g cashew nuts
½ lime

Cook the noodles in a saucepan of boiling water according to the instructions on the packet (about 6 minutes). Drain and rinse immediately under cold water.

Dice the tempeh. Seed the pepper and cut into strips. Peel the carrot and cut into sticks. Cut the broccoli into florets. Finely chop the spring onion and chilli. Peel and finely chop the shallot, garlic and ginger. Mix the soy sauce, rice vinegar and maple syrup with 3 tablespoons of water in a small bowl.

Gently fry the shallot in the sesame oil for 2 minutes over medium heat either in a sauteuse pan or a wok. Add the garlic and ginger and gently fry for 2 minutes. Add the pepper, carrot, broccoli, corn, tempeh and cashew nuts and gently fry for 3 minutes, stirring regularly. Add the sauce, cooked noodles, spring onion and chilli. Sauté, stirring constantly, for 2 minutes, until all the ingredients are hot and coated with sauce.

Serve in bowls with a wedge of lime and soy sauce.

TIPS AND VARIATIONS
- Tempeh is a traditional ingredient made from fermented soybeans. It's usually sold as a compact block. It's increasingly available in the fresh food section of organic shops in Asian grocery shops. Alternatively, use diced tofu or even chickpeas.
- You can make this recipe with any type of Asian noodle: wheat noodles, rice noodles, soba, or even konjac noodles. Feel free to adapt it with the vegetables available: cabbage, pak choi, courgette, beans, etc.

BAKSO: INDONESIAN DUMPLING AND NOODLE BROTH

Here's another favourite traditional dish I discovered in Bali. The word *bakso* means 'meatballs' in Indonesian, and they're usually served in a broth with noodles and vegetables. Like *mie goreng*, it's a typical Indonesian street food that can be bought in *warungs* and from street vendors. Today, there are over twenty variations of *bakso*; this one is made with soft mushroom dumplings and an aromatic noodle broth.

GLUTEN-FREE

SERVES 2
PREP TIME: 30 MINUTES
COOKING TIME: 40 MINUTES
RESTING TIME: 30 MINUTES

FOR THE DUMPLINGS
160 g white mushrooms
1 garlic clove
1 shallot
1 tbsp olive oil
100 g cooked white beans
40 g rolled oats
20 g cornflour
2 tbsp soy sauce
1 tsp maple syrup
½ tsp garlic powder
¼ tsp ground cumin
Salt and pepper

FOR THE BROTH
1 shallot
1 garlic clove
5 g fresh ginger
1 small piece lemongrass
120 g pak choi (or Chinese
  cabbage)
500 ml vegetable stock
1 tbsp sesame oil
6 tbsp coconut milk
2 tbsp soy sauce
10 g dried shiitake or dried
  mushrooms (optional)
1 pinch salt
80 g wheat or rice noodles

FOR DECORATION
1 spring onion
4 sprigs fresh coriander
20 g roasted peanuts
2 tbsp fried onions

Wash and finely chop the mushrooms, garlic and shallot. Heat the oil in a saucepan and gently fry for 5 minutes.

Rinse and drain the beans. Whiz the beans, rolled oats, cornflour, soy sauce, maple syrup, garlic powder and cumin with salt and pepper to a smooth paste. Add the cooked mushrooms and whiz briefly to retain some texture. Cover with cling film in direct contact and leave in the fridge for 30 minutes.

Take 1 tablespoon of the mixture and roll it between your hands into a golf ball-sized ball. Repeat until you have 8 balls. Heat a generous amount of water in a saucepan. When the water comes to the boil, add the dumplings and cook for 15 minutes or until they rise to the surface. Use a skimmer to take them out and drain.

Peel and chop the shallot, garlic, ginger and lemongrass. Pound the aromatics with a mortar and pestle or whiz to a paste. Chop the pak choi. Mix the sesame oil, aromatic paste and pak choi in a saucepan and gently fry for 3 minutes. Next, pour in the stock, coconut milk and soy sauce, then add the dried mushrooms and a pinch of salt. Cover and leave to simmer for 15 minutes. Add the noodles and cook for the time indicated on the packet. Take the saucepan off the hob and keep the broth hot.

Chop the spring onion and coriander and crush the peanuts. Serve the hot noodle broth in bowls with the dumplings and garnished with spring onion, coriander, peanuts and fried onions.

FOR
SHARING

PROVENÇAL AÏOLI WITH AL DENTE VEGETABLES

A great classic of Provençal cuisine, it's perfect for a meal with friends (but don't eat it before a date … you'll understand why!). Originally, aïoli was a mayonnaise-like sauce made from an emulsion of garlic and olive oil. It goes well with fish and seafood, croutons or al dente vegetables. A simple, quick and hearty recipe to share as an appetiser.

GLUTEN-FREE

SERVES 6
PREP TIME: 20 MINUTES
COOKING TIME: 20 MINUTES

FOR THE VEGETABLES
180 g new potatoes
6 small baby carrots
200 g cauliflower
120 g green beans
1 white onion
12 cherry tomatoes
12 pink radishes

FOR THE CROUTONS
1 baguette
1 garlic clove
Olive oil

FOR THE AÏOLI
2 cloves garlic
150 ml soy cream
3 tbsp cider vinegar
1 tbsp mustard
¼ tsp salt
¼ tsp ground pepper
60 ml rapeseed oil
60 ml olive oil

Peel the potatoes and carrots (keep the skin on if they're organic). Cut the cauliflower into florets. Top and tail the green beans. Peel and slice the onion. Steam or boil the vegetables for 15–20 minutes for the carrots, potatoes and cauliflower, and 10 minutes for green beans and onion. Drain the vegetables and cover to keep them warm.

Cut the baguette into slices and brush with oil. Peel the garlic clove and rub it over each slice of bread. Place the bread slices in a dry frying pan and toast for a few minutes on each side.

Peel and crush the garlic. Put the garlic, soy cream, vinegar, mustard, salt and pepper into a tall container and whiz with a stick blender. Gradually pour in the oils as you whiz to emulsify the sauce until it's firm and smooth, like mayonnaise. Set aside in the fridge.

Arrange the vegetables in a large dish and serve with the aïoli sauce and croutons.

TIPS AND VARIATIONS
Add other raw or cooked vegetables: courgette, beetroot, artichokes, fennel, endive, etc.
Serve this dish with tapenade, hummus or tomato caviar (see recipe p. 134).

ROCKET AND PISTACHIO PESTO MINI-BABKAS

Do you enjoy chocolate and orange babka? Here's a savoury version that's just as delicious! These little babkas are made of a soft brioche dough stuffed with a rocket, basil and pistachio pesto that smells like the South of France. As they're small, they're ideal with an aperitif, for lunch with a fresh salad or to take on a picnic.

FOR 6 MINI-BABKAS
PREP TIME: 30 MINUTES
RESTING TIME: 2 HOURS 15 MINUTES
COOKING TIME: 30 MINUTES

FOR THE BABKA DOUGH
110 ml warm almond milk
4 g dried baker's yeast
200 g T55 wheat flour
10 g coconut (or cane sugar)
½ tsp salt
3 tbsp olive oil
Zest ½ lemon

FOR THE PESTO
30 g rocket leaves
20 g toasted pistachios
20 g chopped walnuts
2 tbsp nutritional yeast
1 garlic clove
1 small bunch fresh basil
1 tbsp olive oil
1 tsp balsamic vinegar
1 pinch fleur de sel

FOR DECORATION
10 g dry-roasted pistachios
Neutral oil

FOR THE GLAZE
2 tbsp olive oil
1 tsp maple syrup
½ garlic clove, crushed
1 pinch fleur de sel

Warm the almond milk and pour into a bowl. Sprinkle the yeast over it and leave to activate for 5 minutes, then stir to dissolve.

Combine the flour, sugar and salt in the bowl of a food processor or a large bowl. Make a well in the centre and pour in the milk and yeast mixture, oil and lemon zest. With a food processor: knead with a hook attachment for 5–8 minutes until the dough is smooth and elastic and no longer sticky. By hand: mix with a spatula to incorporate the ingredients, then place the dough on a lightly floured worktop and knead by hand for at least 10 minutes until smooth, elastic and no longer sticky. Roll the dough into a ball and place in an oiled bowl. Cover with a tea towel. Put in a warm place and leave to rise for about 1 hour 30 minutes, or until doubled in volume.

Place all the ingredients for the pesto in a food processor and pulse to a consistently grainy paste (do not whiz it to a smooth consistency as you want some texture).

Roll the dough out on a floured worktop to a rectangle about 60 cm long. Spread the pesto over the entire surface and top with coarsely chopped toasted pistachios. With the long side parallel to you, roll up the dough to form a long sausage, then cut it into 6 equal pieces. Cut each piece in half lengthwise and braid the two halves, passing one length over the other in succession. Seal the ends by pressing them together with your fingertips. Place the babkas in oiled mini loaf tins. Cover with a tea towel and leave to rise for 45 minutes in a warm place.

Preheat the oven to 175°C (gas mark 3-4). Make the glaze by mixing all the ingredients. Bake for 25 minutes. Brush the babkas with the glaze and bake for another 5 minutes, until nicely browned. Take the babkas out of the oven and brush with more glaze. Leave to cool completely before unmoulding.

HERB CRACKERS, HUMMUS, TAPENADE AND TOMATO CAVIAR

Aperitifs are synonymous with crackers and dips. But the next time you have guests over, you can tell them that you prepared everything! This recipe for crunchy herb biscuits goes perfectly with a sun-dried tomato caviar with walnuts, a briny black olive tapenade and a creamy lemon hummus.

GLUTEN-FREE

SERVES 6
PREP TIME: 30 MINUTES
COOKING TIME: 20 MINUTES

FOR THE CRACKERS
100 g oat flour
100 g brown rice flour
60 g cornflour
40 g ground linseed
2 tsp ground cumin
3 tbsp dried rosemary
1 tsp garlic powder
½ tsp salt
3 tbsp olive oil
2 tbsp sesame seeds
1 tbsp poppy seeds
½ tsp fleur de sel

FOR THE TOMATO CAVIAR
40 g sun-dried tomatoes
40 g walnuts
2 tbsp tomato paste
1 tbsp olive oil
1 tbsp balsamic vinegar
½ tsp dried oregano
½ tsp paprika
1 pinch ground chilli
Salt and pepper

FOR THE TAPENADE
100 g black olives
1 garlic clove
5 g capers in brine
1 tbsp olive oil
3 sprigs fresh thyme
1 sheet nori seaweed
Salt and pepper

FOR THE HUMMUS
130 g cooked chickpeas
40 g thick non-dairy yoghurt
1 preserved lemon
½ garlic clove
1 tbsp tahini
1 tbsp olive oil
1 tbsp lemon juice
½ tsp ground cumin
Salt and pepper

Preheat the oven to 165°C (gas mark 3).

Combine the oat flour, rice flour, cornflour, flaxseeds, cumin, 1 tablespoon of the rosemary, garlic powder and salt in a bowl. Stir in the oil. At this stage, the dough should be dry and crumbly. Stir in 140 ml of water until smooth and very slightly sticky.

Shape the dough into a ball and roll it out between two sheets of parchment paper to a thickness of about 3 mm. Sprinkle the dough with sesame seeds, poppy seeds, the remaining rosemary and fleur de sel. Gently roll with the rolling pin so that the seeds and rosemary are embedded in the dough. Use a knife to score small squares on the surface of the dough, making sure you don't cut all the way through. Place the dough on a baking tray and bake for 15 minutes. Now, separate the crackers, turn them over and put them back in the oven for a further 5 minutes, until golden brown. Leave to cool.

Whiz all the ingredients for the tomato caviar to a consistently grainy texture. Don't whiz it to a smooth consistency as you want some texture.

Pit the olives. Peel and chop the garlic. Whiz all the ingredients of the tapenade to a consistent texture.

Rinse and drain the chickpeas, then whiz all the ingredients for the hummus until creamy.

Arrange the tomato caviar, tapenade and hummus on a large platter and serve with the crackers.

TIPS AND VARIATIONS
- For an ultra-creamy hummus, cook dried chickpeas yourself and skin them before whizzing.
- You can also make the tapenade with green olives.

TORTILLA DE PATATAS WITH CREAMY ROASTED PEPPERS

If you go to a bar in Spain, you can be sure to find a *tortilla de patatas* at the top of the tapas menu. This thick egg and potato dish can be eaten as a main course, or cut in small pieces. To add a touch of originality to this simple dish, I add slices of apple and serve it with a delicious roasted pepper cream. Go on, chill the sangria!

GLUTEN-FREE

SERVES 6 TO 8
PREP TIME: 20 MINUTES
COOKING TIME: 60 MINUTES

FOR THE TORTILLA
400 g potatoes
1 Golden Delicious apple
1 yellow onion
2 tbsp olive oil
150 g chickpea flour
70 g plain soy yoghurt
2 tbsp nutritional yeast
½ tsp turmeric
¼ tsp kala namak salt
Salt and pepper

FOR THE PEPPER CREAM
2 large red peppers
1 tbsp olive oil
1 garlic clove
20 g thick non-dairy yoghurt
1 tbsp balsamic vinegar
½ tsp paprika
Salt and pepper

Preheat the oven to 180°C (gas mark 4). Grease and line a rectangular baking tin about 26 × 20 cm with parchment paper.

Peel and cut the potatoes and apple into slices about 2 mm thick using a mandoline. Peel and thinly slice the onion.

Gently fry the potatoes in a frying pan with 1 tablespoon of the oil for 10 minutes over medium heat, without browning, and stirring regularly. Add the apple and onion slices and cook gently for 2 minutes without browning. Season to taste.

Mix the chickpea flour, yoghurt, remaining oil, yeast, turmeric and salt with 200 ml of water to a smooth lump-free batter. Transfer the batter to a bowl and stir in the potato and apple slices. Pour the mixture into the tin in an even layer, so that the slices lie flat, and bake for 20 minutes. Check for doneness by inserting a knife into it: it should sink in without any resistance. Allow to cool in the dish.

Increase the oven temperature to 200°C (gas mark 6). Place the whole peppers on a baking tray and drizzle with oil, then bake for 30 minutes, until tender and the skin is crumpled and brown patches appear. Take out of the oven and cover with a tea towel or aluminium foil and leave to cool for 20 minutes before gently peeling off the skin. Remove the stems and seeds as well.

Peel and chop the garlic. Whiz the peppers, garlic, yoghurt, vinegar and paprika with salt and pepper to a smooth cream. Taste and adjust the seasoning.

Unmould the cooled tortilla, cut into wedges and serve with the pepper cream.

QUICK PISSALADIÈRE FOR SPUR-OF-THE-MOMENT APPETISERS

No, a pissaladière is not a pie, it's a pizza! The word 'pissaladière' comes from the Italian *pizza all'Andrea*, which refers to this speciality made with bread dough topped with meltingly soft onions cooked for a long time in olive oil. Another simple and tasty dish that can be eaten either warm or cold, for lunch or with an aperitif. This gluten-free version is quick to prepare and there's no need to let it rise.

GLUTEN-FREE

SERVES 6
PREP TIME: 30 MINUTES
COOKING TIME: 35 MINUTES

FOR THE DOUGH
120 g coconut milk
1 tbsp olive oil
1 tsp cider vinegar
1 tsp baking powder
½ tsp garlic powder
½ tsp dried oregano
¼ tsp salt
60 g white rice flour
60 g ground almonds
60 g cornflour

FOR DECORATION
300 g yellow onion
2 tbsp olive oil
1 tbsp cane sugar
2 sprigs fresh thyme
6 large black olives
Salt and pepper

Mix the coconut milk, oil and vinegar in a bowl. Add the baking powder, garlic powder, oregano and salt. Mix and leave to stand for 2 minutes: the baking powder will react to the acidity of the vinegar and cause the mixture to froth. Then whisk in the rice flour, ground almonds and cornflour to a fluid, consistent lump-free dough. At this stage, the dough should be slightly moist and sticky, but malleable. Leave at room temperature for 5 minutes.

Peel the onions and slice thinly. Heat the oil in a frying pan, add the onions, sugar and a pinch of salt. Cook the onions gently for 15-20 minutes, stirring regularly, until soft. Add the thyme, increase the heat and gently fry for 2 minutes to brown the onions, stirring to prevent them from burning. Season to taste.

Preheat the oven to 180°C (gas mark 4). Spread the dough on a baking tray lined with parchment paper into a disc about 8 mm thick. Create a rim around the edge. Spread the cooked onion over the dough, leaving some space around the edge, and add the olives. Brush the rim of the dough with oil and bake for 12 minutes, until the rim is golden. Leave to cool for a few minutes before serving.

TIPS AND VARIATIONS
This gluten-free quick dough base can also be used to make thin-crust pizzas or tarts. For example, top with tomato sauce, cream, tapenade or hummus and add vegetables (mushrooms, courgette, aubergine, pepper, etc.).

NACHOS, BROCCOLI GUACAMOLE, PICO DE GALLO AND CHEESE SAUCE

Crunchy, plain or spicy, tortilla chips are the ideal thing for dipping in any kind of sauce, and of course in guacamole. In Mexico and Costa Rica, where the avocados are sublime, I can't remember starting a meal without a basket of tortilla chips and a bowl of guacamole. Here, we have so much beautiful produce that it would be a shame not to revisit it with cooked broccoli. The result is just as creamy and delicious.

GLUTEN-FREE

SERVES 8
PREP TIME: 30 MINUTES
COOKING TIME: 40 MINUTES
RESTING TIME: 1 HOUR

FOR THE TORTILLA CHIPS
4½ tbsp coconut oil
100 g coconut flour
90 g ground almonds
30 g ground flaxseeds
2 tsp garlic powder
1 tsp turmeric
1 tbsp paprika
Salt

FOR THE BROCCOLI GUACAMOLE
200 g broccoli (stem and head)
50 g thick non-dairy yoghurt
1 garlic clove
4 sprigs fresh coriander
1 tbsp lemon juice
½ tsp ground cumin
Salt and pepper

FOR THE CHEESE SAUCE
200 g tinned white beans
4 tbsp nutritional yeast
1 tsp mustard
1 tsp olive oil
1 tsp maple syrup
½ tsp garlic powder
¼ tsp turmeric
Salt and pepper

FOR THE PICO DE GALLO
1 tomato
¼ mango
1 red onion
1 small sweet chilli
4 sprigs fresh coriander
Juice and zest ½ lime
Salt and pepper

Preheat the oven to 160°C (gas mark 3). Melt the coconut oil.

Combine the coconut flour, ground almonds, ground flaxseeds, garlic powder, turmeric and salt in a bowl. Pour in the melted coconut oil and mix. At this stage, the dough should be dry and crumbly. Gradually add 140 ml of warm water until you have a smooth, very slightly sticky dough.

Shape the dough into a ball and roll it out between two sheets of parchment paper to a thickness of about 2 mm. Score strips and then triangles, making sure you don't cut all the way through. Place the dough on a baking tray and bake for 15 minutes. Now, separate the nachos, turn them over and put them back in the oven for a further 5 minutes, until golden brown. Immediately sprinkle the nachos with paprika and salt on both sides (use a brush or kitchen paper) and leave to cool.

Steam or boil the broccoli for 15–20 minutes until tender. Drain and whiz with the remaining guacamole ingredients to a silky cream.

Rinse and drain the white beans before whizzing them with the remaining cheese sauce ingredients to a smooth creamy consistency. If it's too thick, add a little milk.

Dice the tomato and mango. Peel and finely chop the onion, chilli and coriander. Combine all the ingredients for the pico de gallo in a bowl. Refrigerate for at least 1 hour before serving.

TIPS AND VARIATIONS
You can also serve tortilla chips in a large dish, topped with melted non-dairy cheese, guacamole and chilli, like Mexican nachos.

ROUGAIL AND VEGETABLE ACHARD AS MADE IN LA RÉUNION

Rougail is a reflection of Réunion Island: colourful, spicy and with lots of flavour. In my opinion, it's the most emblematic condiment of the island. It's unthinkable to eat a curry, rice, or any other dish without a little rougail on the side. Perhaps you're familiar with the famous rougail sausage, but rougail is actually a condiment made from fruit and vegetables. Although there are several varieties; my favourite, as you may have guessed, is pistachio rougail made with peanut butter, as my mother used to make it.

SERVES 4 TO 6
PREP TIME: 40 MINUTES
RESTING TIME: 48 HOURS
COOKING TIME: 15 MINUTES

FOR THE VEGETABLE ACHARD
½ white cabbage
4 carrots
250 g fresh green beans
½ lemon
1 onion
2 cloves garlic
3 cm fresh ginger
1 or 2 green chillies (to taste)
½ tsp coarse salt
2 tbsp olive oil
1 tsp turmeric
1 tsp ground cumin
1 tbsp vinegar
1 tbsp lemon juice

FOR THE TOMATO ROUGAIL
250 g tomatoes
1 spring onion stalk
2 shallots
2 cm fresh ginger
1 or 2 red chillies (or to taste)
1 pinch fleur de sel
1 tbsp olive oil
Zest ¼ of kaffir lime (or lime)

FOR THE ROUGAIL
1 large yellow onion
1 small bird's eye chilli (to taste)
3 whole peeled tinned tomatoes
1 tbsp olive oil
80 g peanut butter
¼ tsp salt

Thinly slice the cabbage. Peel, wash and julienne the carrots. Top and tail the beans and cut them in half. Slice the lemon. Peel and chop the onion, garlic and ginger. Finely chop the chilli. Pound the onion, garlic, ginger, chilli and salt with a mortar and pestle to a paste.

Blanch the beans in a saucepan of boiling water for 2 minutes before draining and immediately running under cold water.

Heat 1 tablespoon of the oil in a large sauté pan. Add the onion paste, turmeric and cumin and gently fry for 2–3 minutes, stirring. Add the vegetables and cook over high heat for 3 minutes, stirring regularly.

Tip the mixture into a bowl and add the vinegar, lemon juice and remaining oil. Knead with your hands to soften the vegetables and release their juice. Transfer the achard to a jar, close and macerate in the fridge for at least 48 hours.

Finely dice the tomatoes. Finely chop the spring onion. Peel and finely chop the shallots, ginger and chilli. Pound the ginger, chilli and salt with a mortar and pestle. Combine the tomatoes and the ginger-chilli paste in a bowl. Add the oil, spring onion and lime zest and mix. Set aside in the fridge.

Peel and finely chop the onion and chilli. Crush the peeled tomatoes. Gently fry the onion in a frying pan in the oil for 2 minutes without browning. Add the tomatoes and chilli, cook for 5 minutes and then add the peanut butter, 2 tablespoons of water and the salt. Stir and simmer gently for 2 minutes. The rougail should be creamy. Add a little water, a spoonful at a time, to get the right consistency. Leave to cool and set aside in the fridge before serving.

RÉUNIONESE CHILLI BONBONS

Don't be fooled by the name: in Réunion, sweets are not sweet, but fried and spicy. Yet they're so addictive that I could greedily snack on them all the time! These chilli bonbons are similar to falafel, made with lima beans, spices, with (just) a little chilli. You can find them almost everywhere, at roadside stalls, in restaurants, in markets ... in fact it's often my first stop when I return to the island!

FOR 12 CHILLI BONBONS
PREP TIME: 20 MINUTES
SOAKING TIME: OVERNIGHT
COOKING TIME: 20 MINUTES

200 g dried chickpeas (or dry
  lima beans)
1 garlic clove
2 cm fresh ginger
1 or 2 chillies (to taste)
1 spring onion
3 sprigs fresh coriander
2 tsp ground cumin
2 tsp turmeric
1 tsp ground coriander
¼ tsp ground pepper
½ tsp salt
Frying oil (sunflower, peanut, etc.)

Put the chickpeas into a bowl with at least twice their volume of cold water and soak overnight.

The next day, drain the chickpeas and dry them carefully with kitchen paper before whizzing to a fairly dry, grainy purée.

Peel and finely chop the garlic and ginger. Chop the chilli, onion and coriander. Whiz with the chickpea purée, turmeric, ground coriander, pepper and salt. The mixture should be easy to shape.

Take 1 tablespoon of the mixture and roll it between lightly dampened hands and shape into a ball, pressing it well to make it compact. Flatten it slightly and make a hole through the centre with the end of a wooden spoon. Hold the mixture in the palm of your hand to stop it from crumbling.

Fill a saucepan with oil (at least 8 cm) and heat to 180°C. Immerse the bonbons in the oil in small batches of 2–3 and fry for about 4 minutes, until golden on both sides. Drain on kitchen paper.

TIPS AND VARIATIONS
- Chilli bonbons are traditionally made with lima beans. I've adapted this recipe and use chickpeas, which are more readily available. However, if you can find dry lima beans, I encourage you to make the real Réunionese recipe!
- Here are some important tips for making successful chilli bonbons:
    - it's essential to use dried chickpeas (or lima beans) — and not tinned —which you simply soak in water;
    - make sure the oil has reached 180°C before frying the bonbons (check the temperature with a kitchen thermometer and adjust the heat to maintain it throughout the cooking process);
    - fry the bonbons long enough to make the outside dry and crispy (start with frying one as a test).

sweet potato, peanut and MANGO SAMOSAS

Because of my Réunionese origins and the island's South Asian and Far Eastern influences, samosas are etched in my memory. As a child, we ate them on every occasion: sometimes at home, at parties, or in Chinese restaurants. But my best samosa memory comes from my recent trips to Réunion. It's a very popular dish there. My favourite? The peanut butter ones, of course!

GLUTEN-FREE

MAKES 10 SAMOSAS
PREP TIME: 30 MINUTES
COOKING TIME: 45 MINUTES

300 g sweet potato
1 yellow onion
1 garlic clove
1 tbsp fresh ginger
1 stick lemongrass
100 g mango
10 g desiccated coconut
2 tbsp soy sauce
2 tbsp peanut butter
1 tsp turmeric
1 tsp ground cumin
1 pinch salt
3 sprigs fresh coriander
20 g roasted peanuts
5 sheets brik or filo pastry
Olive oil

Peel and chop the sweet potato. Steam or cook in a saucepan of boiling water for about 20 minutes, until tender. Drain and mash with a fork or potato masher.

Peel and finely chop the onion and garlic. Peel and finely chop the lemongrass. Peel and finely dice the mango.

Heat 1 tablespoon of olive oil in a frying pan and gently fry the onion for 2 minutes. Add the garlic, ginger and lemongrass and gently fry for a further 2 minutes over medium heat. Add the mashed sweet potato, mango, coconut, soy sauce, peanut butter, turmeric, cumin and salt. Mix by lightly crushing the mixture with a spatula. Cook for 3 minutes. Remove the saucepan from the hob and add the chopped coriander and crushed peanuts.

Preheat the oven to 180°C (gas mark 4) and line a baking tray with parchment paper.

Cut the sheets of pastry in half and fold them into strips. Place 1 spoonful of filling at the end of a strip, fold the end of the sheet over the filling and then fold over several times into a triangle. Very lightly moisten the end and press gently to seal. Arrange the samosas on the baking tray and brush with olive oil. Bake for 10 minutes, then turn the samosas over and bake for another 5 minutes. Serve the golden crispy samosas with a sauce or condiment.

TIPS AND VARIATIONS
Samosas are a popular dish in many cultures and are made in a range of flavours. Of course, you can swap the sweet potato for potato, but you can also use petit pois, green beans or diced carrots. Feel free to play with spices: curry, five-spice mix, paprika, garam masala, etc.

EMPANADAS STUFFED WITH CHILLI AND POTATOES

Of Hispanic heritage, this is another little culinary treasure! Empanadas, those delicious little stuffed parcels, originated in Spain in the 16th century and spread rapidly to Latin America with the Spanish conquest. They became hugely popular and are an emblematic dish in many countries, including Argentina. Fillings can include vegetables, cheese or meat: the possibilities are endless.

MAKES 10 EMPANADAS
PREP TIME: 40 MINUTES
RESTING TIME: 30 MINUTES
COOKING TIME: 45 MINUTES

FOR THE DOUGH
200 g T55 flour
4 g dried baker's yeast
¼ tsp salt
60 g vegan margarine
85 ml plain soy milk

FOR THE FILLING
300 g sweet potato
50 g red pepper
1 red onion
2 tbsp tomato paste
2 tbsp soy sauce
1 tsp smoked paprika
¼ tsp chilli or ground pepper
100 g tinned kidney beans
60 g tinned sweetcorn
4 sprigs fresh coriander
Olive oil
Salt and pepper

FOR THE GLAZE
3 tbsp soy milk
1 tbsp olive oil
1 tsp maple syrup

Combine the flour, yeast and salt in a bowl. Melt the margarine. Make a well in the centre and add the milk and melted margarine. Mix to incorporate all the ingredients, then knead the dough for 10 minutes on a floured worktop until smooth, elastic and no longer sticky. If, after 5 minutes, it's too sticky, add a little flour. If, on the other hand, it's too dry and firm, add a little milk, 1 teaspoon at a time. Shape into a ball, wrap in cling film and refrigerate for 30 minutes.

Preheat the oven to 180°C (gas mark 4) and line a baking tray with parchment paper. Peel and dice the sweet potatoes. Arrange on the baking tray and drizzle with olive oil. Bake for 20 minutes until tender.

Seed and dice the pepper. Peel and finely chop the onion. Heat 1 tablespoon of oil in a frying pan, add the onion and pepper and gently fry for 5 minutes. Add the sweet potato, tomato paste, soy sauce, paprika, chilli and season. Mix by mashing the sweet potato with a spatula to make a purée. Then add the beans, corn and chopped coriander and mix. Leave to cool.

Raise the oven temperature to 200°C (gas mark 6). Roll out the dough on a floured worktop to a thickness of about 2 mm. Using a cookie cutter or a glass, cut out discs about 10 cm in diameter. Collect the scraps, shape into a ball, roll out again and cut out more discs.

Place 1 tablespoon of filling in the centre of a disc and fold in half to make a small parcel. To seal, carefully pinch the edges with your fingers and use a fork to mark the edges. Transfer the empanadas to a baking tray lined with baking parchment. Make the glaze by mixing the milk, oil and maple syrup, then gently brush the empanadas with it. Bake for 20 minutes, until nice and golden. Take the baking tray out of the oven and brush the empanadas again with the glaze. Leave to cool for 10 minutes before serving.

CRISPY CAULIFLOWER NUGGETS WITH CHIMICHURRI SAUCE

In Argentina, more than just a Sunday meal with friends, barbecuing is a culinary art and a national dish. On my journey through this incredible country, I saw steaming barbecue stands set up along the streets. They start setting up very early in the morning, and there are queues to try the best *asados* in the region! This is also where I discovered chimichurri, a fresh punchy condiment made with herbs and chillies. The perfect sauce to add a bit of spiciness to crispy cauliflower nuggets.

GLUTEN-FREE OPTION

SERVES 4 (TO SHARE)
PREP TIME: 20 MINUTES
COOKING TIME: 25 MINUTES

**FOR THE CAULIFLOWER
 NUGGETS**
80 g thick non-dairy yoghurt
30 ml non-dairy milk
1 tbsp mustard
30 g chickpea flour
1 tsp garlic powder
¼ tsp salt
35 g cornflakes
250 g cauliflower (about ½ head)
25 g panko (or regular
 breadcrumbs, gluten-free if
 necessary)

FOR THE CHIMICHURRI SAUCE
½ bunch of fresh parsley
1 spring onion
1 small piece green chilli
½ shallot
1 garlic clove
2 tbsp lemon juice
2 tbsp olive oil
1 tbsp balsamic vinegar
Salt and pepper

FOR THE YOGURT SAUCE
60 g plain soy yoghurt
1 tsp maple syrup
Juice and zest ½ lime
1 pinch salt

Preheat the oven to 200°C (gas mark 6) and line a baking tray with parchment paper.

Mix the yoghurt, milk, mustard, chickpea flour, garlic and salt in a bowl to a fluid lump-free batter. Crush the cornflakes and combine with the breadcrumbs in a shallow dish.

Separate the cauliflower into medium-sized florets. Dip the florets in the batter to coat completely, then dip in the breadcrumbs before placing them on the baking tray. Bake for 25 minutes, until golden and crispy.

Rinse and very finely chop the parsley, onion and chilli. Peel and finely chop the shallot and garlic. Mix all the ingredients for the chimichurri sauce in a bowl. Taste and adjust the seasoning if necessary. Set aside in the fridge.

Prepare the yoghurt sauce by mixing all the ingredients in a small bowl.

As soon as they're done, serve the cauliflower nuggets with the chimichurri sauce, yoghurt sauce, a turn of the pepper mill and a pinch of fleur de sel.

TIPS AND VARIATIONS
- This recipe also works well with broccoli, romanesco or any variety of cauliflower. Try using purple and yellow cauliflower for a colourful appetiser.
- These cauliflower nuggets can be eaten with all kinds of sauces: chimichurri, yoghurt, barbecue, ranch, mayonnaise, ketchup, aïoli (see recipe p. 130), pesto, hummus, etc.

ALICIA'S TACOS, SHREDDED JACKFRUIT AND MOLE SAUCE

Tacos, burritos, fajitas, quesadillas, enchiladas, nachos... it's amazing what you can make from just corncobs! The taco is the famous tortilla folded over itself to hold a filling, which you then eat with your hands. The most popular are *tacos al pastor*, filled with marinated, shredded pork, and it's become an institution in Mexico. Here are my tacos, with shredded jackfruit, served with a mole sauce.

GLUTEN-FREE OPTION

**MAKES 6 SMALL TACOS
PREP TIME: 30 MINUTES
COOKING TIME: 40 MINUTES**

FOR THE SHREDDED FILLING
250 g jackfruit
45 g tomato paste
25 g soy sauce
1 tbsp maple syrup
1 tbsp balsamic vinegar
1 tsp paprika
¼ tsp ground chilli
1 pinch ground pepper
1 tbsp olive oil

FOR THE SAUCE
½ yellow onion
1 garlic clove
90 g red peppers
80 g tomatoes
1 tbsp olive oil
½ tsp cumin
¼ tsp ground chilli
1 tbsp cocoa powder
30 g pumpkin seeds
10 g tomato paste
1 tbsp lemon juice
Salt and pepper

FOR THE GRILLED CORN
1 corncob
1 tbsp olive oil
1 pinch fleur de sel

FOR DECORATION
6 mini tortillas (gluten-free if
  necessary)
¼ red cabbage
1 avocado
1 green chilli
1 small bunch fresh coriander

Shred the jackfruit into fairly fine pieces. Mix the tomato paste, soy sauce, maple syrup, vinegar, paprika, chilli and pepper in a bowl. Add the shredded jackfruit, mix and marinate for 5 minutes.

Heat the oil in a frying pan. Tip the jackfruit and the marinade into the frying pan and cook over high heat for about 5 minutes, stirring regularly.

Peel and chop the onion and garlic. Dice the peppers and tomatoes. Gently fry the onion in the oil for 2 minutes, then add the garlic, pepper, tomato, cumin and chilli. Cook for 6–8 minutes. Add the cocoa, pumpkin seeds, tomato paste, lemon juice and season. Stir and cook for 2 minutes.

Whiz the mixture until smooth. Taste and adjust the seasoning if necessary. Set aside in the fridge.

Remove the leaves and silk from the corncob and rinse before blanching it for 10 minutes in boiling water, then drain. Heat the oil in a frying pan and fry the corncob for a few minutes all over. Season with salt.

Preheat the oven to 180°C (gas mark 4). Place the mini-tortillas on an oven rack, letting them fall between the bars to form shells, and bake for 6–8 minutes, until the tacos are hard and lightly browned. Leave to cool.

Slice the red cabbage. Scoop the flesh from the avocado and cut into slices. Chop the chilli and coriander. Cut the kernels from the cob. Fill the tacos with the sauce, shredded jackfruit, corn, cabbage and avocado before sprinkling with chilli and coriander.

KOREAN KIMCHI PANCAKES WITH RASPBERRY SAUCE

Pancakes aren't just for breakfast! *Kimchi-jeon* is a popular Korean dish made with kimchi and a flour-based batter. It can be eaten as a snack or for lunch with a bowl of rice, vegetables, a glass of sparkling rice wine and a sweet and sour sauce. Kimchi is a condiment of lacto-fermented vegetables that's a staple of Korean cuisine and is an excellent flavouring for all types of dishes. These original pancakes will surprise your guests and will definitely bring some exoticism to your appetisers!

GLUTEN-FREE

**MAKES 2 LARGE PANCAKES
 (SERVES 6)
PREP TIME: 20 MINUTES
COOKING TIME: 10 MINUTES**

FOR THE RASPBERRY SAUCE
70 g fresh or frozen raspberries
30 g almond butter
2 tbsp soy sauce
1 tbsp balsamic vinegar
1 tsp maple syrup
¼ tsp ground ginger
1 pinch ground chilli (optional)
1 pinch salt

FOR THE PANCAKES
100 g white rice flour
70 g chickpea flour
2 tbsp nutritional yeast
½ tsp turmeric
¼ tsp crushed pepper
1 tsp black salt
80 g kimchi
60 ml kimchi juice
2 spring onions
30 g desiccated coconut
Neutral oil

Whiz all the ingredients for the sauce in a blender until smooth. Taste and adjust the seasoning if necessary. Set aside in the fridge.

Combine the flours with the yeast, turmeric, chilli and salt in a large bowl. Add the finely chopped kimchi, the kimchi juice and 180 ml of water and mix to a smooth lump-free batter. Stir in the chopped spring onions and coconut.

Heat 2 tablespoons of oil in a large non-stick frying pan. Pour in half of the batter and quickly tilt the saucepan to spread the batter over the entire surface. Leave to cook for 2–3 minutes, then carefully turn the pancake over so as not to break it (if necessary, use a plate). Cook the other side for around 2 minutes until the pancake is lightly golden. Repeat with the remaining batter.

Cut the pancakes into wedges and serve immediately with the sauce.

TIPS AND VARIATIONS
Kimchi is a traditional Korean condiment made with lacto-fermented vegetables. They come in many varieties and are made with a range of vegetables and seasonings. The most famous and most common is cabbage kimchi. You can find it in Asian grocery shops and even in some supermarkets. It's made by leaving a mixture of vegetables, spices and seasonings in brine for several weeks. You can also use any variety of lacto-fermented vegetables (carrot, cabbage or beetroot).

BAOZI: STEAMED BUNS STUFFED WITH MUSHROOMS AND KIMCHI

Baozi, a popular Chinese snack, has become the new trend in modern international street food. On the face of it, there's nothing exceptional about these little stuffed steamed buns. But with the first bite, you understand why people go crazy for them! The dough is incredibly soft and light, so it's like biting into a little cloud... Then comes the filling, tender, juicy and fragrant. This version made with mushrooms and kimchi is sure to please.

MAKES 8 BAOZI
PREP TIME: 30 MINUTES
RESTING TIME: 2 HOURS
COOKING TIME: 40 MINUTES

FOR THE DOUGH
10 g fresh baker's yeast (or 4 g
 dry yeast)
10 g caster sugar
250 g T55 flour
½ tsp salt
1 tbsp olive oil

FOR DECORATION
20 g dehydrated black
 mushrooms
60 g cashew nuts
60 g kimchi
150 g brown mushrooms
1 garlic clove
5 g fresh ginger
4 sprigs fresh parsley
1 tbsp olive oil
½ tsp five-spice mix
3 tbsp soy sauce
1 tbsp maple syrup
2 tbsp sesame seeds
1 pinch fleur de sel

Dissolve the yeast and sugar in 150 ml of warm water and allow the yeast to activate for 5 minutes, then stir to dissolve.

Combine the flour, salt, yeast and sugar mixture and olive oil in the bowl of a food processor or in a salad bowl. Knead in a food processor with the hook attachment or by hand on a floured worktop for 10–12 minutes, until the dough is smooth and no longer sticky. Roll the dough into a ball and place in an oiled bowl. Cover with a tea towel and leave to rise in a warm place for about 1 hour and 30 minutes, or until doubled in volume.

Soak the black mushrooms in warm water to rehydrate. Whiz the cashew nuts and kimchi to a paste. Finely chop the brown mushrooms. Peel and chop the garlic and ginger. Chop the parsley. Heat the oil in a sauté pan and sauté the mushrooms for 5 minutes. Add the garlic, ginger and five-spice mix and cook for 2 minutes. Drain and add the black mushrooms and the cashew-kimchi paste. Stir in the soy sauce, maple syrup, parsley, sesame seeds and salt. Mix to obtain the consistency of a pasty stuffing. Set aside in the fridge.

Cut out 8 squares of parchment paper measuring 10 × 10 cm. Flatten the mixture by pressing it with your fist and divide it into 8 pieces weighing about 50 g each. Shape the balls into discs 10 cm in diameter. Place 1 tablespoon of filling in the centre of each disc and fold the edges inwards to form a little bundle. Pinch the top of the dough with your fingers to seal. Place the baozi on the paper squares, cover with a tea towel and leave to rest for 30–40 minutes.

Boil water in a saucepan with a steamer basket on top. When the water comes to the boil, place the baozi and the paper squares in the basket without them touching (2 or 3 baozi at a time depending on the size of the basket). Cover and steam for 10–12 minutes. Lift the lid halfway through cooking to release some of the steam to allow the buns to swell. Leave to cool for a few minutes before serving.

SWEET SNACKS

SOFT CARAMEL, PRETZEL AND HAZELNUT COOKIES

Soft, melt-in-the-mouth, crunchy, stuffed, shortbread, crispy, golden or almost raw ... there are as many ways to enjoy a cookie as there are foodies on Earth. But one thing's for sure, everyone loves them. I could have settled for a traditional American chocolate chip cookie recipe, but I thought it would be crazy to leave out this ultra-decadent version of thick and chewy caramel, hazelnut and pretzel cookies... They're as addictive as they are surprising!

MAKES 14
PREP TIME: 15 MINUTES
RESTING TIME: 3 HOURS 30 MINUTES
BAKING TIME: 12–14 MINUTES

310 g T55 flour
110 g ground almonds
2 tsp baking powder
1 pinch salt
150 g vegan margarine
75 g muscovado sugar
35 g coconut sugar
180 g apple sauce
1 tsp vanilla extract
100 g caramel chocolate buttons
80 g hazelnuts
30 g mini pretzels

Combine the flour, ground almonds, baking powder and salt in a bowl.

Whisk the softened margarine, muscovado sugar and coconut sugar in a bowl until creamy. Add the apple sauce and vanilla and mix well. Pour this mixture over the dry ingredients and mix briefly until the dough is smooth, thick and slightly sticky, then fold in the chocolate buttons, whole hazelnuts and pretzels and mix. Set the dough aside in the fridge for 30 minutes.

Using a tablespoon or ice-cream scoop, scoop out large balls of dough and place on a baking tray lined with parchment paper. The cookies won't spread out much, so there's no need to space them out too much. Leave for 3 hours in the freezer or ideally overnight in the fridge (at worst, 30 minutes in the refrigerator will do).

Preheat the oven to 180°C (gas mark 4) and bake the cookies for 12–14 minutes, until the edges begin to brown. Leave to cool for 20 minutes on the baking tray, then on a wire rack.

TIPS AND VARIATIONS
For perfect cookies:
- to avoid developing gluten bonds that make the cookies elastic, don't overwork the dough;
- put the cookie dough in the fridge before baking; the margarine will harden and the flavours will intensify; the edges will be crispy and the centre will remain soft;
- don't overbake the cookies; ideally, take them out of the oven when they are still a little soft.

LEMON AND BLACK SESAME MUFFINS

Muffins are like mini cakes that definitely aren't for sharing! Little morsels of comfort food and happiness to treat yourself at any time of the day. Like cookies and brownies, these are a kind of sweet pastry that originated in the United States but are now popular all over the world. It's hard to resist their springiness, their delicious flavours and the fact that they're portable. For a change from the classic lemon and poppy seed ones, here are some gluten-free lemon and black sesame muffins.

GLUTEN-FREE

MAKES 6 MUFFINS
PREP TIME: 20 MINUTES
RESTING TIME: 5 MINUTES
COOKING TIME: 20 MINUTES

FOR THE MUFFINS
100 ml plain soy milk
30 ml lemon juice
120 g white rice flour
20 g maize flour
40 g ground almonds
50 g cane sugar
2 tsp baking powder
½ tsp ground cardamom
1 pinch salt
70 g apple sauce
20 g neutral oil (grapeseed,
  peanut, etc.)
Zest 1 lemon
30 g black tahini
10 g black sesame seeds

FOR THE ICING
45 g black tahini
1 tbsp lemon juice
1 tbsp maple syrup
Black sesame seeds
Lemon zest

Preheat the oven to 180°C (gas mark 4) and oil or line muffin tins with parchment paper.

Mix the soy milk and lemon juice in a bowl and leave for 5 minutes.

Combine the rice flour, maize flour, ground almonds, sugar, baking powder, cardamom and salt in a bowl. Add the milk and lemon juice mixture, apple sauce, oil and lemon zest and mix to a smooth batter. Work the tahini and black sesame seeds into a third of the batter (about 150 g).

Divide the white batter between the tins and place a few spoonfuls of black batter on top in the centre. Allow the black batter to spread out over the white one and bake for 20 minutes. Check for doneness by inserting the tip of a knife into the centre of a muffin: it should come out almost dry. Leave to cool for a few minutes before unmoulding. Leave on a wire rack.

Mix the black tahini, lemon juice and maple syrup in a bowl. Top the cooled muffins with icing before sprinkling with sesame seeds and lemon zest.

TIPS AND VARIATIONS
Less well known than the white tahini commonly used in many Mediterranean dishes, such as hummus, black tahini adds flavour and natural colour to your dishes.

THE BEST PEANUT BUTTER AND CHOCOLATE CHIP BANANA BREAD

If there's one cake I love, it's banana bread! Invented during the Great Depression in the United States in the 1930s as a way of using up overripe bananas and reducing waste, it's disconcertingly simple, yet very moist and full of flavour. Definitely a hit as it's become popular all over the world. I haven't visited a country where they don't have it. Now it's my turn to share with you my favourite peanut butter recipe.

GLUTEN-FREE

MAKES 1 LARGE LOAF (ABOUT 10 SERVINGS)
PREP TIME: 15 MINUTES
COOKING TIME: 1 HOUR
RESTING TIME: 1 HOUR 30 MINUTES

3½ tbsp coconut oil
125 ml almond milk
1 tbsp cider vinegar
3 very ripe bananas + 1 not too ripe
50 g peanut butter
1½ tbsp maple syrup
1 tsp vanilla extract
100 g oat flour
100 g brown rice flour
70 g ground almonds
30 g coconut (or cane sugar)
1 tbsp baking powder
1 tsp cinnamon
¼ tsp salt
80 g chocolate chips + some for the topping

Preheat the oven to 180ºC (gas mark 4). Oil and line a 25 × 11 cm loaf tin with parchment paper. Melt the coconut oil.

Mix the almond milk and vinegar in a bowl and leave for 5 minutes.

Peel the ripe bananas and mash coarsely with a fork to a purée. Add the melted coconut oil, peanut butter, maple syrup and vanilla and mix. Stir in the milk and vinegar mixture and mix again.

Mix the remaining ingredients except the chocolate chips and pour over the batter. Work the batter with a spatula, but not too much as you want some texture. Add the chocolate chips, pour the batter into the tin and smooth the surface with the spatula.

Peel and slice the last banana, and arrange the slices on top of the batter. Sprinkle the loaf with a few more chocolate chips and bake for 1 hour. Check for doneness by inserting the tip of a knife into the centre: it should come out almost dry. Cover with foil during baking if the top starts browning too quickly. Leave to cool for at least 30 minutes before unmoulding and wait for at least 1 hour before slicing.

TIPS AND VARIATIONS
Use very ripe bananas as these will bind the batter well and give the cake its sweet taste. They are perfectly ripe when their skin has darkened, has large brown patches and they are soft to the touch.

PROVENÇAL BRIOCHE TARTE DE SAINT-TROPEZ WITH VERBENA AND STRAWBERRIES

This is a typically Provençal brioche where olive oil is used instead of butter. Filled with a verbena-flavoured cream and strawberries, this cake looks like a Tarte de Saint-Tropez and is a wonderful example of the flavours of the South of France.

SERVES 6 TO 8
PREP TIME: 45 MINUTES
COOKING TIME: 30 MINUTES
RESTING TIME: 3 HOURS

FOR THE BRIOCHE PROVENÇAL
6 g fresh baker's yeast
150 g T55 flour
20 g light brown sugar
2 g salt
3 tsp olive oil
Zest ½ lemon

FOR THE GLAZE
1 tbsp agave syrup
5 tbsp soy milk
20 g pearl sugar

FOR THE CREAM
250 ml plain soy milk
10 verbena leaves
50 g caster sugar
30 g cornflour
1 tsp agar-agar powder
200 g thick coconut cream
1 tbsp icing sugar

FOR DECORATION
200 g strawberries

Crumble the fresh yeast into 80 ml of warm water and leave to activate for 5 minutes. Combine the flour, sugar and salt in the bowl of a food processor or in a bowl. Make a well in the centre and pour in the oil, the water and yeast mixture and the lemon zest. Knead in a food processor with the hook attachment or by hand on a floured worktop for 8–10 minutes, until the dough is smooth and no longer sticky. Add a little flour if necessary, and continue kneading. Roll the dough into a ball and place in an oiled bowl. Cover with a tea towel and leave to rise for 1 hour and 30 minutes, or until doubled in volume.

Oil a round spring form baking tin, about 18 cm in diameter. Punch the dough down with your fist. Shape into a ball and place in the tin. Cover and leave to rise for another 40 minutes.

Preheat the oven to 175°C (gas mark 3-4). Mix the agave syrup and soy milk in a small bowl. Brush the dough with glaze before sprinkling with the pearl sugar, then bake for 25 minutes. Allow to cool before unmoulding.

Pour the milk into a saucepan with the verbena leaves and heat for 15 minutes over low heat, then remove the verbena. Mix the sugar, cornflour and agar-agar in a bowl. Add a little hot milk to the dry ingredients, then pour it into the saucepan with the infused milk. Bring to the boil and boil for 3 minutes, whisking constantly until the mixture thickens. Cover with cling film in direct contact and leave to cool at room temperature.

Pour the cold coconut cream and icing sugar into the bowl of a food processor with a whisk attachment. Whisk first on a medium setting, increasing the speed until the cream is firm.

Whisk the cooled pastry cream vigorously until creamy. Add a third of the whipped coconut cream and whisk quickly to loosen it, then fold in the rest with a silicone spatula. Transfer the mixture to a piping bag and refrigerate for 1 hour.

Just before serving, cut the brioche horizontally at ⅔ of its height with a serrated knife. Wash and quarter the strawberries. Arrange the strawberries over the brioche. Pipe the cream between the strawberries and top with the other piece of brioche.

RASPBERRY, PISTACHIO AND WHITE CHOCOLATE MELT-IN-THE-MOUTH BLONDIES

I had planned to give you a classic chocolate brownie recipe, but then a perceptive person pointed out that there's already a lot of chocolate in this book... That's how this incredible raspberry, pistachio and white chocolate blondie is here to delight. This decadent cake is as melt-in-the-mouth as you could wish for, super tasty, easy and quick to make, and just as delicious its famous chocolate cousin. So, are you team brownie or team blondie?

GLUTEN-FREE

MAKES 9 SQUARES
PREP TIME: 15 MINUTES
COOKING TIME: 30 MINUTES
RESTING TIME: 1 HOUR

200 g cooked chickpeas
50 g ground almonds
40 g coconut sugar
2 tsp baking powder
1 pinch salt
200 g almond butter
5 tbsp maple syrup
1 tsp vanilla extract
70 g white chocolate
40 g pistachios
50 g fresh raspberries

Preheat the oven to 180°C (gas mark 4). Oil and line a 20 cm square baking tin with parchment paper.

Rinse and drain the chickpeas. Place, in the following order, the chickpeas, ground almonds, sugar, baking powder, salt, almond butter, maple syrup and vanilla in the bowl of a blender or food processor. Whiz to a smooth thick batter. Pour the mixture into a bowl, then fold in the chopped white chocolate and pistachios by hand.

Pour the batter into the tin in an even layer, then smooth the surface with a spatula. Arrange the raspberries on top, pressing them in very gently, and bake for 25–30 minutes. Check for doneness by inserting the tip of a knife into it. The top of the blondie should be golden brown, but the centre should be soft and gooey. If necessary, cover the blondie with aluminium foil halfway through baking to prevent the chocolate chips from becoming too dark. Leave to cool for at least 1 hour in the tin and then carefully unmould.

TIPS AND VARIATIONS
- You can swap the chickpeas for white beans.
- It's important to use fresh raspberries, as frozen raspberries will release too much water during baking and make the blondie soggy.
- Try making blondies in different flavours that are just as delicious. Here are some of my favourites:
    - dark chocolate and peanut butter;
    - pistachios and fresh apricots;
    - dark chocolate and pecans;
    - cherries, dark chocolate and almonds.

DOUGHNUTS FILLED WITH HOMEMADE APPLE BUTTER AND CARAMEL SAUCE

'Ice cream, doughnuts, cold drinks!' And you're transported to the seaside. Except here, the jam has been swapped for homemade apple butter that's creamy and slightly acidic. Add to this a delicious caramel sauce and you've got doughnuts that can be enjoyed both in summer and winter.

MAKES 12 DOUGHNUTS
PREP TIME: 30 MINUTES
COOKING TIME: 1 HOUR 30
 MINUTES
RESTING TIME: 2 HOURS 25
 MINUTES

FOR THE DOUGHNUT BATTER
145 ml plain non-dairy milk
20 g light brown sugar
10 g fresh baker's yeast
5¼ tbsp coconut oil
250 g T55 flour
4 g salt

FOR THE APPLE BUTTER
600 g apples
30 ml cider vinegar
30 g coconut sugar
1 tsp cinnamon
1 pinch salt
30 g almond butter
1 tsp vanilla extract

FOR THE GLAZE
1 tbsp agave syrup
5 tbsp soy milk

FOR THE CARAMEL SAUCE
20 g almond butter
3 tsp maple syrup
20 ml plain non-dairy milk
1 tsp vanilla extract

Mix the warm milk and sugar in a bowl. Crumble the yeast into the mixture and leave for 3 minutes before mixing well to dissolve. Melt the coconut oil.

Combine the flour and salt in the bowl of a food processor or in a bowl. Make a well and pour in the coconut oil and the milk, sugar and yeast mixture. Knead in a food processor with the hook attachment or by hand on a floured worktop for 8–10 minutes, until the dough is smooth and no longer sticky. Then add a little more flour and continue kneading. Roll the dough into a ball and place in an oiled bowl. Cover with a tea towel and leave to rise for 1 hour and 30 minutes, or until doubled in volume.

Peel the apples and cut the flesh into cubes. Put into a saucepan with the vinegar, sugar, cinnamon and salt. Leave to cook for about 40 minutes over low heat, stirring from time to time, then whiz to a smooth purée. Pour the purée back into the saucepan and cook for a further 20–25 minutes, stirring regularly. When the purée has thickened, remove the saucepan from the hob and add the almond butter and vanilla. Leave to cool, then transfer to a piping bag and set aside in the fridge for 1 hour.

Divide the dough into 12 portions weighing about 40 g each. Shape into balls and place on a baking tray lined with parchment paper. Cover with a tea towel and leave to rise in a warm place for 40 minutes.

Preheat the oven to 180°C (gas mark 4). Mix the agave syrup and soy milk in a small bowl and gently brush the doughnuts with the glaze. Bake for 12–14 minutes, until golden brown. Leave to cool for 15 minutes.

Mix all the ingredients for the caramel sauce in a bowl. Use the tip of a knife to make a small hole in the side of each doughnut. Insert the tip of the piping bag and gently fill the doughnuts with apple butter, taking care not to overfill them. Drizzle the caramel sauce over the doughnuts before eating.

CUSTARD TART WITH PRUNES AND SALTED CARAMEL

The is a dessert that can be found in various forms all over the world: in Great Britain they have custard tart; in Portugal their famous *pastéis de nata*; in China they eat egg tarts; and of course in France they have their famous *flan pâtissier*! This one is a little original as it's a gluten-free version made with buckwheat and prunes, halfway between Far Breton and a pecan pie.

GLUTEN-FREE

SERVES 6
PREP TIME: 40 MINUTES
**BAKING TIME: 1 HOUR 10
  MINUTES**
RESTING TIME: 3 HOURS

FOR THE PASTRY
3 tbsp coconut oil
100 g buckwheat flour
80 g ground almonds
35 g coconut sugar
1 tsp cinnamon
¼ tsp salt
50 ml plain almond milk

FOR THE FILLING
400 g silken tofu
90 g white almond butter
3 tbsp agave (or maple) syrup
1–2 tbsp rum (optional)
1 pinch salt

FOR THE CARAMEL
100 g coconut milk
20 g coconut sugar
1 pinch fleur de sel
1 tsp coconut oil

FOR DECORATION
130 g prunes, stoned
40 g pecan nuts

Preheat the oven to 180°C (gas mark 4). Oil and line a round spring form baking tin, about 18 cm in diameter, with parchment paper. Melt the coconut oil.

Combine the buckwheat flour, ground almonds, sugar, cinnamon and salt in a bowl. Add the coconut oil and milk and mix to a smooth consistency. It should be slightly dry and crumbly but should hold together when pressed between two fingers. If it's too dry, add a little almond milk. Line the baking tin with the pastry, making sure that it reaches a height of about 3 cm. Bake blind for 10 minutes until the pastry is slightly golden. Leave to cool.

Put all the ingredients for the filling into a blender and whiz until smooth. Taste and adjust the amount of syrup and rum if necessary.

Arrange the prunes over the pastry base and pour the filling over them. Gently tap the baking tin on the worktop to remove any air bubbles and smooth the surface. Bake for 30 minutes. Cover the tart with aluminium foil and bake for another 15–20 minutes. Check for doneness by gently tapping the surface of the tart with your finger: it's done when the surface has turned a nice colour, is slightly dry around the edges but still wobbly (but not liquid) in the middle. It will firm up as it cools. Leave the tart to cool at room temperature before placing in the fridge, uncovered, for at least 3 hours or ideally overnight.

Put the coconut milk, coconut sugar and salt into a saucepan. Bring to the boil, then reduce the heat to medium and simmer for 15 minutes until the mixture browns and thickens, stirring regularly. Stir in the coconut oil. Set the caramel aside in the fridge.

Toast the pecans in the oven at 170°C (gas mark 3–4) for 10–12 minutes. Before serving, carefully unmould the tart before drizzling with the caramel sauce and topping with the pecans.

SOFT CHOCOLATE, ALMOND AND ORANGE BLOSSOM BABKA

Babkas have become extraordinarily popular over recent years. However, they're not new: these traditional Eastern European brioches have been enjoyed for centuries. Their name, which means 'grandmother', hails from the shape of the pleated skirts of the women who made babkas for special occasions. Today, they're best known as a braided brioche with a chocolate filling.

SERVES 6 TO 8
PREP TIME: 45 MINUTES
COOKING TIME: 50 MINUTES
SOAKING TIME: 20 MINUTES
RESTING TIME: 2 HOURS 30 MINUTES

FOR THE BRIOCHE DOUGH
200 ml plain non-dairy milk
20 g fresh baker's yeast (or 7 g dry yeast)
350 g T55 flour
60 g coconut sugar
1 tsp cinnamon
2 g salt
5 tbsp olive oil
2 tbsp natural orange blossom flavouring
Zest ½ orange

FOR DECORATION
200 g dates, unpitted
10 g cocoa powder
1 pinch fleur de sel
50 g dark chocolate chips
40 g almonds, roughly chopped

FOR THE GLAZE
1 tbsp maple syrup
5 tbsp soy milk

Crumble the fresh yeast into the warm milk and leave to activate for 5 minutes, then stir to dissolve.

Combine the flour, sugar, cinnamon and salt in the bowl of a food processor or in a bowl. Make a well in the centre and pour in the oil, milk and yeast mixture, orange blossom flavouring and orange zest. Knead in a food processor with the hook attachment or by hand on a floured worktop for 8–10 minutes, until the dough is smooth and no longer sticky. If necessary, add a little more flour and continue kneading. Roll the dough into a ball and place in an oiled bowl. Cover with a tea towel and leave to rise for 1 hour and 30 minutes, or until doubled in volume.

Soak the whole dates in hot water for 20 minutes to soften. Drain, pit and coarsely chop. Whiz the dates, cocoa and salt with 60 ml of water on the highest setting to a smooth paste.

Oil and line a 25 × 11 cm baking tin with parchment paper.

Roll the dough out on a floured worktop to a 25 × 35 cm rectangle. The shorter side of the rectangle should be about the length of the tin. Spread the chocolate filling over the entire surface of the dough with a spatula. Sprinkle with the chocolate chips and almonds, and roll the dough up along the long side, holding it firmly with your hands. Cut the roll in half lengthwise. Place the two halves side by side, cut sides up. Pinch the two ends, then braid the two strands together, passing them over each other. Place the babka in the tin, pressing it gently if necessary. Cover with a tea towel and leave to rise in a warm place for 40 minutes.

Preheat the oven to 170°C (gas mark 3-4). Make the glaze by mixing the maple syrup and milk in a small bowl. Gently brush the babka with glaze and bake for 50-60 minutes until golden brown. Cover with aluminium foil during baking if it browns too quickly. Immediately after removing from the oven, brush the babka with glaze again and leave to rest for 20 minutes in the tin before unmoulding and leaving it to cool on a rack.

COCONUT DULCE DE LECHE ALFAJORES

My memories of Argentina are of its immense wilderness, Patagonia's impressive glaciers, the magical spectacle of whales just off the shore ... and the alfajores! You simply cannot visit South America and not try these little biscuits filled with dulce de leche, either coated in chocolate or rolled in desiccated coconut, or both. From snacks to desserts, any occasion is good for enjoying them. I even made my own birthday cake with them on my trip!

GLUTEN-FREE

MAKES 8 ALFAJORES
PREP TIME: 20 MINUTES
COOKING TIME: 45 MINUTES
RESTING TIME: 1 HOUR

FOR THE DULCE DE LECHE
200 g thick coconut cream
60 g coconut sugar
1 tsp vanilla extract
½ tsp fleur de sel

FOR THE BISCUITS
3½ tbsp coconut oil
50 g oat flour
50 g white rice flour
75 g ground almonds
1¼ tsp baking powder
1 pinch salt
25 g coconut sugar
3 tbsp maple syrup

**FOR THE CHOCOLATE
 COATING**
100 g dark cooking chocolate
1 tbsp coconut oil

Place all the ingredients for the dulce de leche in a saucepan. Bring to the boil, then reduce to medium and simmer for 30 minutes: it will reduce by half and turn into a thick, creamy caramel. Stir regularly to avoid it catching on the bottom of the saucepan. Transfer to a bowl and refrigerate for 1 hour to firm up; this makes it easier to work with.

Preheat the oven to 175°C (gas mark 3-4) and line a baking tray with parchment paper. Melt the coconut oil.

Combine the oat and rice flours, ground almonds, baking powder and salt in a bowl. Mix the coconut sugar, maple syrup and coconut oil in a bowl. Pour the liquid mixture over the dry ingredients and mix to a smooth, slightly dry dough. It should be firm enough to shape without crumbling. If it's too dry, add a little coconut oil and maple syrup.

Shape the dough into a ball and roll it out between two sheets of parchment paper to a thickness of about 5 mm. Using a cookie cutter, cut out discs about 5 cm in diameter. Carefully place the discs flat on the baking tray. Collect the scraps, shape into a ball, roll out and cut out more discs. Bake for 12–14 minutes, until golden. Leave the alfajores to cool on the baking tray to dry and harden.

Melt the chocolate and coconut oil in a bain-marie or in a microwave.

Place 1 spoonful of dulce de leche on one alfajor and gently press another on it so they stick together and the dulce de leche is evenly distributed. Use a spoon to dip the alfajores in the melted chocolate to coat them all over. Place the alfajores on a wire rack and let the chocolate harden at room temperature.

CREAMY CHOCOLATE HUMMUS AND CRUNCHY BISCUITS FOR DIPPING

You're familiar with hummus as an appetiser, but here's a chocolate version! Halfway between a spread and raw biscuit dough, this creamy chickpea hummus is great for a healthy, nutritious and very tasty snack. Enjoy it with these delicious crunchy hazelnut biscuits, fresh seasonal fruit, spread on a slice of bread, with yoghurt and granola, or eat it straight from the bowl!

GLUTEN-FREE

SERVES 4
PREP TIME: 25 MINUTES
RESTING TIME: 1 HOUR
COOKING TIME: 10–12 MINUTES

FOR THE HUMMUS
150 g cooked chickpeas
15 g cocoa powder
2 tbsp maple syrup
30 g tahini
1 tsp vanilla extract
1 pinch salt
30 ml plain non-dairy milk

FOR THE BISCUITS
30 g oat flour
30 g ground hazelnuts
10 g coconut sugar
¾ tsp baking powder
½ tsp cinnamon
1 pinch salt
25 g maple syrup
1¼ tbsp coconut oil
7 g sesame seeds

Rinse and drain the chickpeas. Place, in the following order, the chickpeas, cocoa, maple syrup, tahini, vanilla and salt in the bowl of a food processor or in a bowl or in a blender. Whiz to a smooth thick consistency. Add the milk while whizzing (adjust the amount of milk so that the hummus is smooth). Cover with cling film in direct contact and refrigerate for 1 hour.

Preheat the oven to 175°C (gas mark 3-4) and line a baking tray with parchment paper. Melt the coconut oil.

Combine the oat flour, ground hazelnuts, sugar, baking powder, cinnamon and salt in a bowl. Add the maple syrup, melted coconut oil and sesame seeds and mix to a smooth dough. It should be firm enough to work with without crumbling. Shape the dough into a ball and roll it out between two sheets of parchment paper to a thickness of about 3 mm. Cut into small rectangles to the desired size. Gather the dough scraps, roll into a ball and roll out again to make more biscuits.

Bake for 10–12 minutes, until golden brown, and leave to cool on the baking tray. Once they have cooled, gently lift them off, taking care not to break them.

Serve the chocolate hummus with the biscuits and fresh fruit.

TIPS AND VARIATIONS
Swap the tahini for hazelnut butter for a delicious spread. You can also use kidney beans or white beans instead of chickpeas.

CARROT MUG CAKE AND CREAM CHEESE

What could be more comforting than a freshly baked cake? But we don't always have time to make them. Luckily, this delicious snack is ready in just a few minutes; a delicately spiced, springy carrot mug cake that will warm the cockles of your heart! And because a carrot cake wouldn't be the real deal without icing, here it's served with a silky walnut cream.

GLUTEN-FREE / OIL-FREE

MAKES 1 MUG
PREP TIME: 5 MINUTES
COOKING TIME: 2 MINUTES

FOR THE CREAM CHEESE
30 g macadamia nuts
30 g cashew nuts
1 tbsp maple syrup
1 tsp lemon juice
3–4 tbsp non-dairy milk

FOR THE MUG CAKE
20 g almond butter + a little for
  serving
40 g apple sauce
1 tbsp maple syrup
20 g finely grated carrots
20 g almond (or oat) flour
½ tsp baking powder
½ tsp cinnamon
¼ tsp ground ginger
1 pinch ground nutmeg
1 pinch ground cloves
1 pinch salt
10 g walnut kernels + a few to
  serve
10 g raisins
½ tsp orange zest + a little to
  serve

Whiz the nuts with the maple syrup, lemon juice and 1 tablespoon of milk. Gradually add the rest of the milk and whiz to a smooth cream. Set aside in the fridge.

Mix the almond butter, apple sauce and maple syrup in a microwave-safe mug. It should be large enough to be three-quarters full, as the batter will swell during baking. Add the grated carrots, ground almonds, baking powder, spices and salt and mix until smooth. Stir in the coarsely chopped walnuts, raisins and orange zest.

Bake in the microwave on the highest setting for 90 seconds. Check the cake by tapping it with your finger: it should be springy and slightly dry on top. If the cake is still too moist, cook for another 15 seconds, then check again. Continue in 15-second intervals. Be careful not to cook it for more than 3 minutes to keep the centre molten.

Leave to cool for a few minutes before topping with a generous dollop of cream cheese, a drizzle of almond butter, chopped walnuts and orange zest.

TIPS AND VARIATIONS
- This mug cake can also be baked in a conventional oven for 10–12 minutes at 180°C (gas mark 4).
- You can swap the ground cinnamon, ginger, nutmeg and cloves for 1 teaspoon of carrot cake or gingerbread spice mix.
- If your blender isn't powerful enough to make the cream cheese, you can swap it for 1 spoonful of non-dairy yoghurt mixed with 1 spoonful of maple syrup.

CRUNCHY ALMOND AND ANISEED BISCUITS

The story of these biscuits goes back many years, from a trip to Amsterdam. In a small café I had a simple almond biscuit, the texture and flavour of which were unforgettable. Back in my kitchen, I challenged myself to create the easiest biscuit recipe possible, and with few ingredients. That's how these almond biscuits came about. They're quick and simple to make, soft on the inside and crunchy on the outside. This version embraces the flavours of Provence, but you can make them in a thousand and one ways.

GLUTEN-FREE

**MAKES 9 BISCUITS
PREP TIME: 15 MINUTES
COOKING TIME: 12–14 MINUTES**

4 tbsp coconut oil
20 g almonds
150 g white rice flour
100 g ground almonds
1¼ tsp baking powder
1 pinch salt
5 tbsp maple syrup
1 tsp natural orange blossom
  flavouring
½ tsp bitter almond extract
20 g pine nuts
1 tbsp aniseed

Preheat the oven to 175°C (gas mark 3-4) and line a baking tray with parchment paper. Melt the coconut oil. Set aside 9 almonds and coarsely crush the rest.

Combine the rice flour, ground almonds, baking powder and salt in a bowl. Add the melted coconut oil, maple syrup, orange blossom flavouring and bitter almond extract and mix to a smooth dough. It should be firm enough to shape without crumbling. If it's too dry, add a little coconut oil and maple syrup. Add the almonds, pine nuts and aniseed.

Divide into 9 equal portions and shape them into balls by compacting the dough between your hands. Arrange the balls of dough on the baking tray, spacing them 2–3 cm apart. Using the palm of your hand, gently flatten the balls to form the biscuits. Gently press a whole almond into each biscuit and bake for 12–14 minutes, until golden brown. Leave to cool on the baking tray.

TIPS AND VARIATIONS
This is a very simple and easy recipe to make gluten-free biscuits, which can be made in any number of ways: swap the ground almonds for ground hazelnuts, the orange blossom flavouring for vanilla, the aniseed for chocolate chips, the almonds and pine nuts for hazelnuts, pecans or sunflower seeds... Use spices such as cinnamon, ginger, cardamom, nutmeg or cloves for a comforting gingerbread version.

APPLE, WALNUT AND BUCKWHEAT CRUMBLE WITH TAHINI SAUCE

Crumbles are one of my favourite snacks. I remember a tea room in Toulouse that served an incredible crumble that had big chunks of apple under a (very) generous layer of crumble. It has become my weekend ritual, and savoured with a cup of tea it's a moment of pure comfort. It's that feeling I wanted to convey to you with this delicious apple pudding that's topped with a nut and buckwheat crumble and drizzled with tahini sauce.

GLUTEN-FREE

SERVES 6
PREP TIME: 40 MINUTES
COOKING TIME: 50 MINUTES

FOR THE PASTRY
4½ tbsp coconut oil
80 g white rice flour
50 g chestnut flour
40 g cornflour
80 g ground almonds
30 g coconut sugar
½ tsp salt

FOR THE CRUMBLE
60 g walnuts
50 g hulled buckwheat
30 g rice flour
30 g ground almonds
20 g coconut sugar
1 pinch salt
40 g tahini
2¼ tbsp coconut oil

FOR THE APPLE FILLING
650 g apples (about 4 apples)
30 g coconut sugar
2 tbsp cornflour
2 tbsp lemon juice
½ tsp cinnamon
¼ tsp ground nutmeg

FOR THE TAHINI SAUCE
50 g thick non-dairy yoghurt
30 g tahini
1 tbsp maple syrup
1 tsp vanilla extract

Preheat the oven to 180°C (gas mark 4). Oil the bottom and sides of a high-sided flan dish about 24 cm in diameter. Melt the coconut oil.

Combine the rice and chestnut flours, cornflour, ground almonds, sugar and salt in a bowl. Add the coconut oil and 60 ml of cold water and mix with a spoon to a smooth consistency. It should be slightly crumbly but firm enough to hold together when pressed between two fingers. If it's too dry, add a little water, 1 spoonful at a time, until you achieve the right consistency. Roll out the pastry, line the dish with it and prick the base with a fork. Set aside in the fridge.

Crush the nuts. Mix the nuts, buckwheat, rice flour, ground almonds, sugar and salt in a bowl. Add the tahini and melted coconut oil and mix.

Seed the apples before cutting them in half (keep the skin on if they're organic) and use a mandoline to cut thin slices. Put the apple slices into a bowl and add the sugar, cornflour, lemon juice, cinnamon and nutmeg. Mix gently to coat well. Place the apples in an even layer in the pastry shell. Sprinkle the crumble over the fruit.

Bake for 50 minutes. Cover with aluminium foil after 15 minutes to stop the crumble from browning too quickly. The apples should be tender and the crumble topping golden brown. Leave to cool at room temperature for at least 30 minutes.

Make the tahini sauce by mixing all the ingredients in a bowl. Drizzle the crumble generously with the sauce before serving.

TIPS AND VARIATIONS
- if you're short of time, use a ready-made shortcrust pastry.
- You can adapt your crumble to the time of the year by using seasonal fruit: pears, berries, rhubarb and even tropical fruit such as pineapple or banana.

FLUFFY CRÊPES WITH CHOCOLATE SAUCE

When I was little, my mother often made me crêpes for a snack. I can still remember the cover of the recipe book she used to make them. They were so good that I didn't add anything, not even a little sugar. I hope you'll find this recipe delicious, perhaps plain as it is, but just in case, I serve it with a little chocolate sauce...

MAKES ABOUT 20 CRÊPES
PREP TIME: 20 MINUTES
COOKING TIME: 20 MINUTES
RESTING TIME: 1 HOUR

FOR THE CRÊPE BATTER
400 g T45 flour
60 g cornflour
2 tbsp caster sugar (optional)
¼ tsp salt
950 ml almond milk
30 g neutral oil (grapeseed, peanut or sunflower)
1 tbsp natural orange blossom flavouring
2 tsp vanilla extract

FOR THE CHOCOLATE SAUCE
120 g dark chocolate
200 ml plain non-dairy milk
1½ tbsp maple syrup

Combine the flour, cornflour, sugar (for slightly sweet crêpes) and salt in a bowl. Pour in about a third of the milk at once and whisk vigorously to a smooth, lump-free batter, then gradually whisk in the rest. Add the oil, orange blossom flavouring and vanilla and mix until fluid and lump-free. Cover and leave in the fridge for 1 hour.

Chop the chocolate before putting it into a small saucepan with the milk. Simmer for 6–8 minutes over low heat, stirring regularly. Stir in the maple syrup at the end of cooking.

Lightly oil a frying pan with a piece of kitchen paper and heat it up (it should be hot but not burning). Pour in a ladleful of batter and tilt the pan so it spreads over the entire surface. When the edges start to dry and come away from the pan, flip the crêpe over. Cook for 1 minute on the other side and then slide the crêpe onto a plate. Repeat the process with all the batter, oiling the frying pan as necessary. Cover the cooked crêpes to stop them from drying out.

Serve immediately, topped with chocolate sauce and garnished with whatever ingredients you like.

TIPS AND VARIATIONS
Making crêpes is a piece of cake! Here are a few tips on how to make foolproof batter:
- adjust the amount of milk according to whether you prefer thinner or thicker crêpes (check by dipping the back of a ladle into the batter and running your finger across it: it should leave a clear trace);
- leave the batter to rest in the fridge for at least 1–2 hours or, ideally, overnight: this allows it to strengthen, and the flavours to develop for even tastier crêpes.

desserts

MILLIONAIRE PEANUT AND CARAMEL SHORTBREAD

One bite is enough to understand why it's described as 'millionaire'. With its crunchy shortbread base, melt-in-the-mouth caramel topped with roasted peanuts and a creamy chocolate top layer, these ultra-rich, indulgent Scottish morsels are worth all the gold in the world! Traditionally enjoyed for afternoon tea, they're simply perfect with a good cup of tea.

GLUTEN-FREE

MAKES 9 SQUARES
PREP TIME: 30 MINUTES
BAKING TIME: 15 MINUTES
RESTING TIME: 1 HOUR 20 MINUTES

FOR THE SHORTBREAD
5¼ tbsp coconut oil
150 g coconut flour
2 tbsp maple syrup
1 tsp vanilla extract
1 pinch salt

FOR THE CARAMEL
120 g peanut butter
4 tbsp maple syrup
2¼ tbsp coconut oil
1 tsp vanilla extract
1 pinch fleur de sel
70 g roasted peanuts

FOR THE GANACHE
150 g dark chocolate
30 g peanut butter
1 pinch fleur de sel

Preheat the oven to 180°C (gas mark 4). Oil and line a 20 cm square baking tin with parchment paper.

Melt the coconut oil. Mix the coconut flour, melted coconut oil, maple syrup, vanilla and salt in a bowl to an even, fairly dry and crumbly dough. Place the dough in the tin and press on it firmly with your fingers or with a flat-bottomed object (a glass, jar, etc.) to spread it evenly. Bake for 10–12 minutes, until nice and golden. Leave to cool in the tin.

Put the peanut butter, maple syrup, coconut oil, vanilla and fleur de sel in a small saucepan. Warm it up over very low heat for a few minutes, stirring regularly to thin the mixture. Remove from the hob, add the roasted peanuts, then pour the caramel over the shortbread base. Set aside for at least 1 hour in the freezer to harden.

Coarsely chop the chocolate, then melt it in a bain-marie until fluid. Add the peanut butter and mix to a smooth silky ganache. Pour the ganache over the hardened caramel in an even, smooth layer. Sprinkle with fleur de sel and refrigerate for 20 minutes.

Carefully remove the shortbread from the tin. Heat the blade of a knife under hot running water, dry it and cut the shortbread into neat pieces.

TIPS AND VARIATIONS
If you like, swap the coconut flour for ground almonds, and the peanut butter for almond or cashew butter.

RUSTIC APRICOT TART WITH LEMON AND ROSEMARY-ALMOND CREAM

A last-minute dinner, surprise guests or perhaps you fancy a delicious dessert? Treat your guests to this light rustic fruit tart that's packed with flavour. Made with homemade shortcrust pastry, a silky almond cream and good roasted fruit in syrup, this foolproof recipe is ready in a jiffy and with just a few ingredients. And the best part? You can make it all year round with seasonal fruit!

SERVES 6 TO 8
PREP TIME: 30 MINUTES
BAKING TIME: 35 MINUTES
RESTING TIME: 30 MINUTES

FOR THE SHORTCRUST PASTRY
250 g T55 flour
20 g light brown sugar
¼ tsp salt
50 g olive oil

FOR THE ALMOND CREAM
1 sprig fresh rosemary
80 g soy cream
50 g ground almonds
3 tsp maple syrup
10 g light brown sugar
1 tsp vanilla extract
½ tsp ground cardamom
Zest ½ lemon

FOR THE FILLING
300 g apricots
1½ tbsp maple syrup
1 tbsp lemon juice
1 tsp vanilla extract
3 sprigs fresh rosemary
30 g hulled buckwheat
30 g pine nuts

FOR THE GLAZE
1 tbsp maple syrup
5 tbsp plain non-dairy milk
Light brown sugar
Flaked almonds

Combine the flour, sugar and salt in a bowl. Pour in the oil a little at a time and mix quickly, then gradually add 100 ml of cold water and mix to a dough. Knead the dough for 5 minutes until it's smooth and no longer sticky, but don't overwork it. If it's very sticky and difficult to knead, add a little flour. Shape into a ball, cover with cling film in direct contact, and leave to rest for 30 minutes at room temperature.

Finely chop the rosemary. Mix all the ingredients for the almond cream in a bowl so that it's thick and smooth.

Stone the apricots and cut into medium-thick slices. Mix the maple syrup, lemon juice and vanilla in a small bowl. Put the apricot quarters and rosemary sprigs into a bowl and pour the syrup over them. Mix gently to coat the fruit.

Preheat the oven to 180°C (gas mark 4).

Roll out the dough on a sheet of parchment paper into a disc about 3 mm thick and 30 cm in diameter. With the dough on the parchment paper, transfer it to the baking tray. Spread the almond cream over it, leaving a 3 cm or so edge all around. Arrange the apricots and rosemary on it and pour all the syrup over it. Sprinkle with the buckwheat and pine nuts. Fold the edges of the pastry towards the centre of the tart, partially covering the filling.

Make the glaze by mixing the maple syrup and milk. Brush the folded edges of the tart with the glaze, then sprinkle with light brown sugar and flaked almonds. Bake for 30–35 minutes until the pastry is nicely caramelised and the apricots roasted. Leave to cool for a few minutes on the baking tray before serving the tart with a scoop of vanilla ice cream.

LEBANESE RICE CUSTARD PUDDING WITH ORANGE BLOSSOM, ROSE AND PISTACHIOS

Mouhallabieh is a light, aromatic Lebanese pudding flavoured with orange blossom. Very easy to prepare, this dessert is traditionally made with milk, sugar and cornflour. This is an equally easy and delicious version made with rice. When whizzed, the cooked rice – that's high in starch – gives these little puddings an incredibly light silky texture. Enjoy them chilled, drizzled with a delicate rose syrup and garnished with a few toasted pistachios.

GLUTEN-FREE

MAKES 4 SMALL PUDDINGS
PREP TIME: 15 MINUTES
RESTING TIME: 1 HOUR
COOKING TIME: 20 MINUTES

FOR THE FLAN
85 g uncooked basmati rice
320 ml plain almond milk
2 tbsp agave or maple syrup
2 tbsp natural orange blossom
 flavouring
1 pinch salt
1 tsp agar-agar powder

FOR THE DECORATION
6 tbsp maple syrup
1 tsp rosewater
1 handful toasted pistachios
Dried rose petals

Rinse the rice before cooking it with two parts boiling water to one part rice for 12–15 minutes. Cook until tender and the rice has absorbed all the water. Remove the saucepan from the hob, cover and leave to swell for 2 minutes.

Put the rice, almond milk, agave syrup, orange blossom flavouring and salt in a blender and whiz until very smooth. Add the agar-agar and whiz again. Transfer to a saucepan and bring to the boil. When the mixture starts boiling, lower the heat and simmer for 2 minutes, whisking constantly. Divide the cream between 4 verrines or ramekins and leave to cool at room temperature before setting aside in the fridge for at least 1 hour.

Mix the maple syrup and rosewater in a small bowl.

Just before serving, take the puddings out of the fridge, drizzle with the syrup and top with a few roasted pistachios and rose petals.

TIPS AND VARIATIONS
Agar-agar is a natural plant-based gelling agent made by drying and pulverising algae. A very good alternative to animal-sourced gelatin, it has been used for centuries in Japanese desserts. Readily available in shops, it comes in various forms: powder, flakes, bars or strands. The most common form (and easiest to use in my opinion) is powder. To activate the gelling action of agar-agar, it's important to incorporate it evenly into a mixture and then heat it for at least 2 minutes.

TRIPLE CHOCOLATE BROWNIE MOUSSE CAKE

Three layers, three textures, three flavours, and three times as much chocolate for three times as much pleasure! This indulgently chocolatey cake has a rich and melt-in-the-mouth hazelnut brownie layer, a creamy chocolate custard, a light mousse and a chocolate chip topping. Watch out, molten chocolate cake! You've got competition...

GLUTEN-FREE

SERVES 6 TO 8
PREP TIME: 40 MINUTES
BAKING TIME: 20 MINUTES
RESTING TIME: 5 HOURS

FOR THE BROWNIE BASE
120 g tinned kidney beans
30 g oat flour
20 g ground hazelnuts
20 g cocoa powder
30 g coconut sugar
1½ tsp baking powder
1 pinch salt
50 g hazelnut butter
30 ml plain non-dairy milk
1 tsp vanilla extract

FOR THE MIDDLE LAYER
100 g dark chocolate
40 g cornflour
1 tsp agar-agar powder
300 ml plain almond milk
100 ml non-dairy cream
2 tbsp maple syrup
1 tsp vanilla extract

FOR THE MOUSSE
100 g dark chocolate
150 g silken tofu
100 g thick non-dairy yoghurt
1½ tbsp maple syrup
1½ tbsp coconut oil
1 pinch salt

FOR DECORATION
100 g dark chocolate shavings

Preheat the oven to 180°C (gas mark 4). Oil and line a round spring form baking tin, about 18 cm in diameter, with parchment paper.

Put the brownie base ingredients – in the order shown on the left – into the jar of a blender or the bowl of a food processor and whiz to a thick smooth batter. Pour the batter into the tin in an even layer. Smooth the surface and bake for 18 minutes. Leave to cool in the tin.

Chop the chocolate. Dissolve the cornflour and agar-agar in a little milk, then pour the mixture into a saucepan with the remaining milk, the cream, maple syrup and vanilla. Heat over low heat until simmering and cook for 3 minutes, whisking constantly until the mixture thickens and is smooth. Remove the saucepan from the hob, add the chopped chocolate and stir to melt. Pour the cream into the tin and spread it evenly over the brownie, then set aside in the fridge for 1–2 hours.

Chop the chocolate, then melt in a bain-marie. Whiz the tofu, yoghurt, maple syrup and salt. Add the melted chocolate and whiz until mixed in. Melt the coconut oil, add to the mixture and whiz for 1 minute to emulsify.

Pour the mousse over the hardened middle layer and smooth the surface, or use a spatula to make a pretty pattern. Set aside for 3 hours in the fridge.

Carefully unmould the cake and sprinkle with chocolate shavings before serving.

TROPICAL COCONUT, MANGO, PASSION FRUIT AND PUFFED RICE BARS

Halfway between a chocolate bar and a dessert, these light and airy, mouth-watering pretty tropical-flavoured bars might very well awaken the pastry chef in you! Made with a no-bake macadamia nut biscuit base, a mango and passion fruit cream and a silky coconut cream, they're coated in crispy white chocolate and puffed rice. Delicate fruity flavours to make your taste buds travel!

GLUTEN-FREE

MAKES 10 BARS
PREP TIME: 40 MINUTES
COOKING TIME: 10 MINUTES
RESTING TIME: 3 HOURS

FOR THE BISCUIT BASE
180 g rolled oats
140 g macadamia nuts
3 tbsp coconut oil
2 tbsp maple syrup
1 pinch salt

**FOR THE MANGO AND
PASSION FRUIT CREAM**
70 g passion fruit (approx. 8 fruit)
200 g fresh mango
60 g coconut milk
15 g cornflour
1–2 tbsp agave syrup (optional)

FOR THE COCONUT CREAM
1 vanilla pod
240 ml plain almond milk
200 g coconut cream
4 g agar-agar powder
30 g agave syrup
3¾ tbsp coconut oil

FOR THE COATING
30 g puffed rice
250 g white chocolate
2–3 tbsp coconut oil

Whiz the rolled oats and macadamia nuts to very small grains. Melt the coconut oil and add it together with the maple syrup and salt. Whiz briefly to an even consistency. Line small rectangular moulds measuring about 9 × 4 cm with cling film. Place the dough inside and press firmly with your fingers to create an even layer. Press the centre of the dough with your fingertips to make a small cavity. Set aside in the fridge.

Scoop out the pulp and juice from the passion fruit. Peel the mango and cut it into pieces. Whiz the passion fruit, mango, coconut milk and cornflour. Pour into a small saucepan and heat for 5 minutes over low heat, stirring until the mixture thickens. Taste and add a little agave syrup if necessary. Transfer the cream to a piping bag and set aside in the fridge.

Split the vanilla pod in half and scrape out the seeds. Whiz the milk, coconut cream, agar-agar and vanilla seeds. Pour into a saucepan, bring to the boil and cook for 3 minutes over low heat, stirring constantly. Pour into a bowl and leave to cool.

Then whiz the cream again to make it creamy. Melt the coconut oil and pour it into the cream while continuing to whiz to emulsify the mixture. Transfer the cream to a piping bag and refrigerate for 30 minutes. Pipe the mango and passion fruit cream into the cavity in the centre of the moulds, then pipe the coconut cream to fill them to the top. Sprinkle the bars with puffed rice and freeze for 2 hours.

Chop the white chocolate and melt it in a bain-marie. Add 2–3 tablespoons of coconut oil. Carefully unmould the frozen bars before dipping them in the melted chocolate. Place the bars on a rack or in a dish and set aside in the fridge for 20 minutes.

MY CHILDHOOD'S CHOCOLATE-RASPBERRY ICE CREAM

When I was a child, one of my favourite summer desserts was to mix two flavours of ice cream into a single cream. The flavours merged and the slightly warm ice cream was smooth and soupy. Here, we're talking about two distinct ice creams, a chocolate and hazelnut one that's super-smooth and luscious, and a raspberry one that's fruity and refreshing. The two are a perfect match in this easy-to-make frozen dessert, whether you have an ice-cream maker or not.

GLUTEN-FREE

SERVES 4 TO 6
PREP TIME: 20 MINUTES
RESTING TIME: 2 HOURS
SOAKING TIME: 10 MINUTES

**FOR THE CHOCOLATE-
 HAZELNUT ICE CREAM**
160 g dates (unpitted)
100 g hazelnut butter
25 g cocoa powder
300 g coconut cream
1 tsp vanilla extract

**FOR THE RASPBERRY
 ICE CREAM**
100 g frozen raspberries
200 g frozen banana slices
100 g coconut milk
1 tbsp maple syrup
½ tsp ground cardamom
1 tsp vanilla extract

FOR DECORATION
Dark chocolate
Roasted hazelnuts

Soak the whole dates in hot water for 10 minutes to soften. Pit the dates before whizzing them on the highest setting with the hazelnut butter, cocoa, coconut cream and vanilla until smooth and creamy. With an ice-cream maker: pour into the ice-cream maker and churn for 1 hour, then set aside in the freezer. Without an ice-cream maker: pour the cream into a container and set aside in the freezer. Stir every 30 minutes until the ice cream has the desired texture.

Whiz the raspberries, banana, coconut milk, maple syrup, cardamom and vanilla until smooth. Taste and adjust the amount of maple syrup if necessary. Set aside in the freezer as you did with the chocolate ice cream.

Pour one third of the raspberry ice cream into a tray or airtight container. Cover with a third of the chocolate-hazelnut ice cream, and continue alternating the two. Sprinkle with little pieces of chocolate and crushed hazelnuts. Leave in the freezer for at least 1 hour before serving.

TIPS AND VARIATIONS
Swap frozen raspberries for blueberries, blackcurrants, strawberries or frozen mango.

HAZELNUT PRALINES

If there's one thing I love more than anything else during the festive season, it's these little praline chocolate truffles. Their comforting flavour, melt-in-the-mouth centre and crunchy coating make them the perfect treat to enjoy and to give as a gift. Lighter than the famous shop-bought version but just as delicious, here's my quick and easy recipe for praline 'rochers' with hazelnut butter. Don't forget to bury a hazelnut in the middle! They're guaranteed to be unforgettable.

GLUTEN-FREE

MAKES 10 PRALINES
PREP TIME: 30 MINUTES
RESTING TIME: 2 HOURS 20
 MINUTES

FOR THE HAZELNUT CREAM
50 g dark chocolate
60 g coconut cream
60 g hazelnut butter
3 tsp maple syrup
10 g unsweetened cocoa
1 tsp vanilla extract
1 pinch fleur de sel

FOR THE COATING
60 g dark chocolate
1 tbsp coconut oil
20 g roasted hazelnuts
15 g cocoa nibs

FOR THE FILLING
10 roasted hazelnuts

Coarsely chop the chocolate and melt in a bain-marie until liquid.

Mix the coconut cream, hazelnut butter, maple syrup, cocoa, vanilla and salt in a bowl. Add the melted chocolate and stir until smooth and silky. Cover and set aside in the fridge for 2 hours (or 30 minutes in the freezer).

Coarsely chop the chocolate and melt in a bain-marie with the coconut oil, stirring until completely combined. Crush the roasted hazelnuts before mixing them with the cocoa nibs in a bowl.

When the cream has firmed up, scoop out 1 tablespoon of dough and shape into a disc with your hands. Place a hazelnut in the centre and roll the dough into a ball between your hands, warming it a little to soften. Roll the balls in the crushed hazelnut and nib mixture to coat all over, dip immediately in the melted chocolate. Set aside for 20 minutes in the fridge to allow the coating to harden.

TIPS AND VARIATIONS
- This recipe makes a perfect year-end gift.
- You can also roll the balls in desiccated coconut, crushed pistachios or almonds, or sprinkled with cocoa powder, matcha tea or freeze-dried raspberry powder after dipping them in the melted chocolate.

AMAZING BANOFFee CHeeSecaKe

When I started my plant-based cooking adventure, I used to make a different cheesecake every Friday. It was a learning experience and a relaxing, as well as a great way to express my creativity. I can't tell you how many flavour combinations I've experimented with over the years, but this banoffee cheesecake is one of my favourites. With a shortbread base, a silky banana cream, topped with a date caramel, it's a light, revisited version of this famous British dessert.

GLUTEN-FREE

SERVES 8
PREP TIME: 40 MINUTES
RESTING TIME: 3 HOURS
COOKING AND BAKING TIME:
 30 MINUTES
SOAKING TIME: 20 MINUTES

FOR THE BASE
70 g oat flour
40 g ground almonds
30 g cane (or coconut) sugar
1 tsp cinnamon
½ tsp salt
3 tbsp coconut oil
3 tsp maple syrup

FOR THE CHEESECAKE FILLING
1 tin coconut milk
100 g raw cashew nuts
2 very ripe bananas
1 tbsp coconut oil
40 g agave syrup
1 tbsp lemon juice
¼ tsp salt
1½ tbsp coconut oil

FOR THE CARAMEL
100 g dates, pitted
120 ml coconut milk
1 tsp vanilla extract
¼ tsp salt

FOR DECORATION
30 g coconut flakes
30 g dark chocolate
1 banana

Chill the coconut milk in the refrigerator overnight.

Preheat the oven to 180°C (gas mark 4). Oil and line a round spring form baking tin, about 18 cm in diameter, with parchment paper.

Combine the flour, ground almonds, sugar, cinnamon and salt in a bowl. Melt the coconut oil. Add the melted coconut oil and maple syrup to the dry ingredients and mix to a smooth dough. It should be slightly dry and crumbly, but firm enough to work with. Place the dough in the tin and press firmly with your fingers or using a flat-bottomed object (a glass, jar, etc.) to spread it evenly. Bake for 10 minutes, until lightly golden. Leave to cool.

Soak the cashews in hot water for 20 minutes, then rinse and drain. Peel the bananas and cut into thick slices. Heat 1 tablespoon of coconut oil in a frying pan and gently fry the bananas for 3–5 minutes, stirring regularly to caramelise.

Open the tin of coconut milk and take 90 g from the layer of cream that's formed on the top. Whiz the cashews, roasted bananas, coconut cream, agave syrup, lemon juice and salt to a smooth cream. Melt the coconut oil and pour it into the cream while continuing to whiz.

Pour the cream into the tin and spread evenly with a spatula. Gently tap the tin on the worktop to remove any air bubbles and smooth the surface. Cover and set aside in the freezer for at least 3 hours.

Soak the dates in hot water for 20 minutes to soften. Drain the dates, pit them and chop the flesh. Whiz the dates, coconut milk, vanilla and salt with 30 ml of water until smooth and silky. Pour the mixture into a saucepan. Bring to the boil, then simmer for 10 minutes over medium heat until the mixture reduces and darkens. Stir regularly to prevent the caramel from burning. Set aside in the fridge.

Spread the coconut chips on a baking tray and toast at 180°C (gas mark 4) for 3–4 minutes. Keep a close eye on them to prevent from burning.

Use a potato peeler to make chocolate shavings. Peel and slice the banana.

When ready to serve, carefully remove the cheesecake from the tin before drizzling with the caramel sauce and topping it with the banana slices, toasted coconut chips and chocolate shavings. Leave the cheesecake to warm up for 10 minutes at room temperature before serving.

DESSERTS

TIPS AND VARIATIONS
You can prepare the caramel without dates by following the recipes for custard tart (see recipe p. 172) or alfajores (see recipe p. 176).

CITRUS TRIFLE, COCONUT CHANTILLY CREAM AND CARAMELISED POPCORN

A good trifle is a joyful marriage of textures, colours and flavours. This comforting and festive typically English dessert consists of layers of cream, sponge cake and fruit. This version has everything you could wish for in a dessert. It has the perfect softness of the sponge cake, the sweetness of the coconut Chantilly cream, the tangy freshness of the citrus fruits and the deliciousness of the caramelised popcorn.

SERVES 4
PREP TIME: 40 MINUTES
RESTING TIME: 1 HOUR
BAKING TIME: 35 MINUTES

FOR THE SPONGE CAKE
75 g thick non-dairy yoghurt
45 ml non-dairy milk
25 g neutral oil
40 g coconut sugar
1 tsp vanilla extract
70 g T55 wheat flour
25 g ground almonds
1¼ tsp baking powder
1 pinch salt
½ tsp ground ginger
Zest ½ lime

FOR THE COCONUT CHANTILLY CREAM
300 g coconut cream
1 tbsp caster sugar

FOR THE CARAMELISED POPCORN
20 g almonds
Neutral oil
15 g popping corn
2 tbsp + 1 tbsp maple syrup
15 g almond butter
1 tsp vanilla extract
1 pinch fleur de sel
1 pomelo or grapefruit
Zest ½ lime

FOR THE DECORATION
1 orange
1 pomelo or grapefruit
1 tbsp maple syrup
1 pinch vanilla seeds
Zest ½ lime

Preheat the oven to 180°C (gas mark 4) and line a baking tray with parchment paper.

Put the ingredients for the sponge cake into a large bowl. Stir to a smooth and even batter, without overworking it. Pour the batter into the baking tray in an even layer about 1.5 cm thick and bake for 12–14 minutes, until the sponge is dry and springy to the touch. Remove the sponge cake from the oven, cover with a tea towel and leave to cool.

Prepare the Chantilly cream. Open the tin of chilled coconut cream and remove only the thick layer from the top. Put that cream topping into the bowl of a food processor with the sugar and whiz at first on the medium setting, gradually increasing it until the cream is frothy and firm. Set the Chantilly cream aside in a piping bag.

Toast the almonds in the oven at 170°C (gas mark 3–4) for 12 minutes. Leave to cool for a few moments before crushing.

Pour enough oil into a saucepan to cover the bottom and heat over medium heat. Add the popping corn and cover. Cook until the corn begins to pop, shaking the saucepan to ensure it cooks evenly. When all the corn has popped, remove the lid and tip the popcorn into a bowl. Add the crushed toasted almonds.

Pour 2 tbsp of maple syrup into a small saucepan. Bring to the boil, then lower the heat and simmer for 2 minutes, stirring. Remove the saucepan from the hob and add the almond butter, vanilla extract and salt. Pour over the popcorn and mix. Spread the popcorn and almonds on a baking tray lined with parchment paper and bake for 7 minutes at 180°C (gas mark 4). Leave to cool completely.

Peel the oranges and grapefruit and remove the segments by cutting next to the membrane and then lifting out the supremes. Do this over a bowl to catch the juice. Put the supremes in the juice and add 1 tablespoon of maple syrup, the vanilla seeds and lemon zest.

Just before serving, cut the sponge cake into cubes. Pipe a layer of Chantilly cream into a glass coupe. Arrange the sponge cake cubes and citrus fruit supremes on top before piping more Chantilly cream over them. Repeat to form several layers. Top with popcorn and caramelised almonds.

TIPS AND VARIATIONS
- The sponge cake and Chantilly cream can be prepared in advance.
- This dessert is a great way to use up leftover cake. You can swap the sponge cake for pieces of cake, muffins or even biscuit crumbs!

MONT BLANC CREAMS WITH CARAMELISED BUCKWHEAT AND HAZELNUT CRUNCH

Those white mountains in the windows of pastry shops have always fascinated me. They look so airy, elegant and intriguing with their generous dome of chestnut cream vermicelli. It makes you want to stick a spoon in to see what's underneath. When I delved deeper into the subject, I learnt that this dessert has two origins: French and Caribbean. A bit like me, actually! Perhaps that's why I wanted to offer you my recipe that has a silky vanilla cream and a caramelised hazelnut and buckwheat crunch.

GLUTEN-FREE

MAKES 4 CREAMS
PREP TIME: 30 MINUTES
RESTING TIME: 1 HOUR
BAKING TIME: 20 MINUTES

FOR THE CHESTNUT CREAM
150 g plain cooked chestnuts
2 tbsp maple syrup
90 ml plain non-dairy milk
1 tsp vanilla extract

FOR THE VANILLA CREAM
1½ tbsp coconut oil
400 g silken tofu
40 g almond butter
2 tbsp agave (or maple) syrup
1 pinch ground vanilla

FOR THE CRUNCH
40 g hulled buckwheat
40 g peeled hazelnuts
30 g caster sugar

Put the ingredients for the chestnut cream into a blender and whiz to a smooth, thick lump-free cream. Set the cream aside in a piping bag in the fridge.

Melt the coconut oil. Put the tofu, almond butter, agave syrup and vanilla into the blender and whiz to a smooth cream. Gradually add the coconut oil while continuing to whiz. Divide the mixture between small verrines or ramekins and refrigerate for at least 1 hour.

Toast the buckwheat and whole hazelnuts in the oven at 170°C (gas mark 3–4) for 12–15 minutes, or in a frying pan over medium heat for about 10 minutes, stirring regularly. Leave to cool and then crush the hazelnuts.

Tip the sugar into a small, heavy-bottomed saucepan. Heat dry until it melts and browns. Don't stir the caramel as it will crystallise! If necessary, tilt the saucepan slightly to distribute the caramel over the entire bottom of the saucepan. When it's a nice colour, add the toasted buckwheat and hazelnuts and mix to coat. Pour it out onto a worktop or silicone mat and leave to cool completely. Hot caramel can burn so be careful when handling it.

Just before serving, pipe the chestnut cream over the vanilla cream and sprinkle with pieces of the crunchy caramelised topping.

TIPS AND VARIATIONS
Making dry caramel can be a little tricky the first time. Here are some rules to follow to get it right:
- use white or light brown sugar (whole or unrefined sugars such as coconut sugar don't work as well);
- make sure your saucepan is dry and clean to avoid any impurities or water ruining the caramel;
- don't stir the sugar during the whole caramel-making process;
- if you have a sweet tooth, beware: do not lick the spoon! Just-made caramel is very hot. Let it cool down before you touch it.

COCONUT-MANGO MILK STICKY RICE ROLLS AND PEANUT SAUCE

Mango sticky rice is one of the most typical and delicious desserts in Thai cuisine. It's made with rice and served with sweetened coconut milk and fresh mango. A dessert that's very easy to make with just a few ingredients, but incredibly delicious! And when this Thai dish is merged with Vietnam's famous spring rolls, the result is rice rolls dipped in an irresistible peanut butter sauce.

GLUTEN-FREE

MAKES 6 ROLLS
PREP TIME: 30 MINUTES
SOAKING TIME: 30 MINUTES
COOKING TIME: 20 MINUTES

FOR THE STICKY RICE
200 g glutinous (sticky) rice
150 g coconut milk
1 piece fresh ginger
3 green cardamom pods, crushed
20 g coconut sugar
1 pinch salt

FOR THE ROLLS
½ mango
6 sheets rice paper
12 fresh mint leaves

FOR THE PEANUT SAUCE
40 g peanut butter
1 tbsp maple syrup
1 tbsp coconut milk
1 tbsp lime juice
1 tsp vanilla extract
Zest ½ lime

Soak the rice in cold water for 30 minutes, drain and rinse several times until the water runs clear. Put the rice into a saucepan with 200 ml of water. Bring to the boil, then reduce the heat to low, cover the saucepan and cook gently for 10 minutes without removing the lid. When all the water has been absorbed, remove the saucepan from the hob and leave for 10 minutes, still with the lid on.

Pour the coconut milk into a small saucepan. Add the sliced fresh ginger, cardamom, sugar and salt. Heat and stir to dissolve the sugar, then remove the saucepan from the hob and leave to infuse for 10 minutes. Strain the milk through a sieve before pouring it into the cooked rice. Stir well. Leave to cool completely.

Peel the mango and cut into thin slices. Pour hot water into a large dish and moisten the surface of your chopping board. Dip a sheet of rice paper completely in the hot water for a few seconds and shake gently with your fingers to soften it. Spread the rice paper on the chopping board. Place two mint leaves and a few mango slices on one side of the rice paper. Place 3 spoonfuls of sticky rice on top to make a sausage shape. Fold the rice paper over and partially roll it up, pressing the filling together gently, taking care not to pierce the paper. Fold in the edges and finish rolling. Repeat with remaining rice paper. Place the rolls in a lightly moistened dish and set aside in the fridge.

Prepare the peanut sauce by mixing all the ingredients in a bowl. Serve the rolls chilled and dip in the sauce.

TIPS AND VARIATIONS

- This recipe can be adapted by replacing the mango with fresh seasonal fruit: strawberries, kiwi, banana or pear slices.
- Making these rolls may seem tricky the first time! Here are some tips on how to get it right:
- gather all the ingredients so that you have them on hand for easy assembly;
- make sure to moisten your chopping board and hands to stop the paper from sticking;
- don't overfill the rolls, as this will make it hard to roll them up;
- finally, you might want to watch a video on the internet before you start!

SPICED, DRIED FRUIT STICKY TOFFEE PUDDINGS

England, Scotland and Ireland all argue fiercely about the origin of this deliciously moist cake made with dates. I have to admit it's addictive! Between the dates, the caramel sauce poured over it and the scoop of ice cream it's topped with, this pudding is an irresistible temptation. I'd like to invite you to discover – or rediscover – this lovely little cake in an equally delicious, but much lighter version. However, you cannot forego the scoop of vanilla ice cream!

GLUTEN-FREE

MAKES 4 PUDDINGS
PREP TIME: 30 MINUTES
COOKING AND BAKING TIME:
 50 MINUTES
RESTING TIME: 20 MINUTES

FOR THE PUDDINGS
150 g dates
80 g raisins
360 ml plain almond milk
40 g almond butter
1½ tbsp maple syrup
170 g oat flour
2½ tsp baking powder
2 tsp cinnamon
1 tsp ground ginger
¼ tsp salt
40 g pecan nuts, coarsely
 chopped

FOR THE TOFFEE SAUCE
1 tin coconut milk
40 g coconut sugar
3 tbsp maple syrup
¼ tsp salt
4½ tbsp coconut oil

FOR THE TOPPING
Vanilla ice cream
Pecan nuts

Chill the coconut milk in the fridge overnight.

Preheat the oven to 180°C (gas mark 4). Oil and line muffin tins with parchment paper.

Pit the dates and chop coarsely. Place the dates, raisins and almond milk in a saucepan. Heat gently until simmering, then cook for a further 5 minutes. Remove the saucepan from the hob, cover and leave to infuse for 20 minutes.

Whiz the milk and the dried fruit until smooth. Add the almond butter and maple syrup and whiz again.

Combine the oat flour, baking powder, cinnamon, ginger and salt in a bowl. Pour the cream over the dry ingredients and mix to a batter. Stir in the coarsely chopped pecans and spoon the batter into the tin. Bake for 20 minutes, until the puddings are dry to the touch but still gooey in the middle. Leave to cool for 10 minutes before unmoulding.

Open the can of coconut milk and take 240 g from the layer of cream that's formed on the top. Put the cream, sugar, maple syrup and salt into a saucepan. Bring to the boil and then simmer for 15 minutes over low heat, stirring regularly. Remove the saucepan from the hob and add the coconut oil. Stir to melt. Keep it hot and, if necessary, gently reheat the sauce before serving if it's too thick.

When ready to serve, drizzle the warm puddings with the sauce before topping with a scoop of vanilla ice cream and pecans.

TIPS AND VARIATIONS
Preferably use large medjool dates and large, plump raisins to give the puddings a melt-in-the-mouth texture and natural sweetness. You can swap the raisins for dried apricots or figs. Soak the fruit in the hot milk to soften it as this makes it easier to whiz.

LIGHTLY SPICED COFFEE TIRAMISÙ

In restaurants in Italy, you'll quite likely be offered tiramisu at the end of your meal. And because you're bound to be tempted, you'll be brought a big dish and it'll be spooned straight onto your plate! Still hungry? Don't worry, here come seconds. I have to say, Italians certainly know how to entertain. And tiramisu is definitely the dish that best embodies Italian generosity and love of sharing. *Tirami sù* literally means 'pull me up', in other words, 'cheer me up'. Mission accomplished with this ultra-creamy dessert and soft spiced sponge cake.

SERVES 6 TO 8
PREP TIME: 40 MINUTES
RESTING TIME: 3 HOURS
COOKING AND BAKING TIME:
 30 MINUTES
SOAKING TIME: 20 MINUTES

FOR THE SPONGE CAKE
150 g thick non-dairy yoghurt
90 ml plain non-dairy milk
50 g neutral oil
60 g coconut sugar
1 tsp vanilla extract
130 g T55 flour
50 g ground almonds
2½ tsp baking powder
1 pinch salt
2 tsp cinnamon
1 tsp ground ginger
¼ tsp ground nutmeg
¼ tsp ground cloves
Zest ½ orange

FOR THE CREAM
150 g cashew nuts
300 g silken tofu
150 g thick non-dairy yoghurt
70 g agave syrup
½ tsp ground vanilla
1 pinch salt
4½ tbsp coconut oil

FOR THE CRUNCHY ALMONDS
40 g almonds
6 g cocoa powder
5 g coconut sugar
3 g ground coffee
1 pinch fleur de sel

FOR THE COFFEE SYRUP
90 ml strong coffee
30 g cane sugar
1 tsp vanilla extract

Preheat the oven to 180°C (gas mark 4) and line a baking tray with parchment paper.

Mix the yoghurt, milk, oil, coconut sugar and vanilla in a bowl. Stir in the remaining sponge cake ingredients to make a smooth batter, without overworking it. Pour the batter onto the baking tray in an even layer about 1.5 cm thick and bake for 12–14 minutes, until the sponge is dry and springy to the touch. Cover the sponge cake with a tea towel to prevent it from drying out and leave to cool.

Soak the cashew nuts in hot water for 20 minutes to soften. Rinse and drain the cashew nuts before whizzing them on the highest setting with the tofu, yoghurt, agave syrup, vanilla and salt until smooth and creamy. Melt the coconut oil and pour it into the cream while continuing to whiz to emulsify the mixture. Transfer the mixture to a piping bag and refrigerate for at least 1 hour.

Toast the whole almonds at 170°C (gas mark 3–4) for about 12 minutes. Leave to cool a little, then whiz until they become like small grains. Mix them with the cocoa, sugar, coffee and salt.

Pour the coffee, sugar and vanilla into a small saucepan. Bring to the boil, then simmer for 5 minutes over low heat to dissolve the sugar. Don't let the syrup reduce too much.

Cut the sponge cake into strips the length of your serving dish. Place strips of sponge cake in the bottom of the dish. Pour a little coffee syrup over the sponge cake, cover with cream, then add a second layer of sponge cake, soak it in syrup and finish with a layer of cream. Set aside for at least 2 hours in the fridge. Sprinkle the tiramisu with the crunchy almonds just before serving.

MATCHA AND SESAME MOCHI STUFFED WITH RED BEAN PASTE

These soft fluffy little clouds are increasingly common now in our pastry shops... Mochi are just like Japan: delicate, refined, light and full of flavour. Filled with a sweet bean paste, mochi are traditionally eaten on special occasions such as New Year's Eve. Originally, they were eaten during the tea ceremony to mellow the delicate bitterness of matcha tea.

GLUTEN-FREE

MAKES 10 MOCHI
PREP TIME: 30 MINUTES
SOAKING TIME: 20 MINUTES
COOKING TIME: 2 MINUTES
RESTING TIME: 30 MINUTES

FOR THE FILLING
65 g dates (about 3 large dates)
150 g cooked kidney beans
50 g hazelnut butter
1 tsp vanilla extract
½ tsp brown miso (or 1 pinch salt)
2 tbsp toasted sesame seeds

FOR THE MOCHI
100 g glutinous rice flour
20 g icing sugar
1 tsp matcha tea powder
40 ml coconut milk
2 tbsp white sesame seeds
2 tbsp black sesame seeds
Cornflour

Soak the dates in hot water for 20 minutes to soften. Drain and pit. Put the rinsed and drained beans, dates, hazelnut butter, vanilla and miso (or salt) into a blender and whiz to a smooth lump-free dough. Add the sesame seeds and whiz briefly. Shape the dough into 10 small balls and freeze for 30 minutes to firm up.

Mix the rice flour, sugar, matcha and coconut milk with 80 ml of water in a microwave-safe bowl. Cover the bowl tightly with cling film and microwave at 850 W for 1 minute and 30 seconds. Remove the cling film and stir. You should now have a thick, malleable and slightly sticky dough. If the dough is still a little runny, cover and cook in 30-second intervals, checking the texture each time.

Take the balls of filling out of the freezer. Mix the white and black sesame seeds. Prepare a small bowl of water. Sprinkle the worktop, a rolling pin and your hands with cornflour.

Take 1 tablespoon of mochi dough, shape it into a ball with your hands and roll it out into a disc. Place the disc in the palm of your hand and put a ball of bean filling in the middle. Fold the edges of the disc over the filling and pinch the dough with your fingers to close it, without leaving any holes. Roll the mochi into a ball. Repeat with the remaining dough to make 10 mochi. When all the mochi have been made, moisten them with a little water and then roll them in the sesame seeds.

Leave the mochi in the fridge for 30 minutes before eating.

TIPS AND VARIATIONS

- Here are some tips on how to shape mochi easily:
    - gather all the ingredients so that you have them on hand for easy assembly;
    - make sure you cook the dough long enough. It's cooked when it becomes opaque;
    - shape the mochi quickly after the dough is cooked, as it dries out rapidly!

CREAMY RICE PUDDING AND COFFEE PRALINE SAUCE

Some desserts, such as rice pudding, are particularly memorable. Perhaps it's because it's deliciousness takes you back to when you were a child? Or maybe it's the creaminess, the hint of vanilla, or simply those memories of childhood and shared moments that it brings back. Whatever the case, this simple and comforting treat will continue to delight us for a long time to come. Rediscover it here, topped with a sweet and savoury coffee praline sauce.

GLUTEN-FREE

SERVES 4 TO 6
PREP TIME: 15 MINUTES
COOKING TIME: 25 MINUTES

FOR RICE PUDDING
200 g short-grain rice
900 ml almond milk
1 tsp cinnamon
1 pinch ground vanilla or 1
 teaspoon liquid vanilla extract
2–3 tbsp maple syrup
½ tsp brown miso (optional)

**FOR THE COFFEE PRALINE
 SAUCE**
60 ml strong coffee (2 espressos)
120 g hazelnut butter
4 tbsp maple syrup
1 pinch salt

FOR THE TOPPING
Toasted hazelnuts
Toasted coconut chips
Cocoa nibs

Pour the milk, cinnamon and vanilla into a saucepan and bring to the boil. When the milk starts to boil, tip in the rice. Wait for the mixture to come back to the boil and then cook for 20–25 minutes over low heat, stirring regularly, until the rice is tender and creamy. If necessary, add a little milk during cooking to achieve the desired consistency.

Mix the hot coffee, hazelnut butter, maple syrup and salt in a bowl until smooth and silky.

When the rice is cooked and very creamy, add the maple syrup and miso (if using) off the heat. Mix in well. Taste and adjust the amount of maple syrup if necessary.

Serve the rice pudding warm in bowls or ramekins, generously drizzled with sauce and garnished with hazelnuts, coconut chips and cocoa nibs.

DESSERTS

TIPS AND VARIATIONS
Rice pudding is traditionally prepared with short-grain rice. Higher in starch than basmati or Thai rice, it becomes slightly sticky while cooking, giving this dessert its super-rich creamy texture. Remember not to rinse it before you cook it! Alternatively, you can use risotto rice (Arborio).

INDEX

A

Aioli 130

Alfajores 176

Almond cheese 95

Almond cream 192

Almond milk 194, 215, 220

Almonds 43, 44, 48, 57, 95, 100, 102, 115, 138, 141, 161, 162, 165, 168, 172, 174, 176, 183, 184, 192, 204, 207, 216

Apple butter 171

Apples 50, 171, 184

Apricots 192

Aubergine 78, 87, 93, 96

Avocado 105, 152

B

Babka 133, 174

Bakso 127

Banana bread 165

Bananas 200, 204

Bánh mì 78

Banoffe cheesecake 204

Baozi 156

Barbecue sauce 70

Beans, green 130, 142

Biscuits 179, 183

Blondies 168

BLT 87

Brioche 167

Broccoli 124, 141

Broth 127

Brownie 196

Buckwheat 210

Buns 70, 77, 78

Burgers 60, 77

Burrito 84

C

Cabbage 122, 142, 152

Caesar sauce 105

Caramel sauce 50, 171, 172, 190

Carrot cake 181

Carrots 78, 100, 116, 130, 142

Cashew nuts 70, 78, 100, 102, 105, 118, 124, 156, 181, 204, 216

Cauliflower 106, 118, 130, 151

Chakchouka 93

Cheese sauce 70, 83, 141

Chestnut cream 210

Chickpea flour 60, 80, 90, 106, 110, 121, 137, 151, 155

Chickpeas 67, 105, 112, 134, 144, 179

Chilli bonbons 144

Chimichurri sauce 151

Chocolate 39, 44, 48, 53, 161, 176, 179, 186, 190, 196, 200, 202, 204

Chocolate chips 57, 165, 174

Chocolate sauce 53, 186

Chocolate spread 54

Chocolate, white 168, 199

Churros 53

Cinnamon 36

Coconut 39, 47, 53, 116, 146, 155

Coconut chantilly cream 207

Coconut cream 167, 176, 199, 200, 202, 207

Coconut milk 40, 43, 44, 77, 78, 83, 112, 116, 118, 127, 138, 172, 199, 200, 204, 213, 215, 218

Coffee praline sauce 220

Coffee syrup 216

Cookies 44, 57, 161

Courgettes 58, 90, 93

Crackers 134

Cream cheese 181

Crêpes 186

Croutons 130

Crumble 184

Cucumber 67, 78, 116, 122

Curry 112, 118

Custard tart 172

D

Dahl 116

Danish pastries 40

Dates 43, 54, 174, 200, 204, 215, 218

Dough 133, 148, 156

Dough, babka 133

Doughnuts 171

Dukkah 96

Dulche de leche 176

E

Empanadas 148

F

Falafel 80

Filo pastry 110, 146

French toast 53

Fries 106

G

Granola 47, 48

Guacamole, broccoli 141

H

Hazelnuts 48, 73, 99, 161, 196, 200, 202, 210, 220

Hot dogs 77

Hummus 62, 87, 134, 179

I

Ice cream 200

J

Jackfruit 152

Jam 54

K

Kale 105, 106

Kidney beans 54, 70, 148, 196, 218

Kimchi 155, 156

L

Leek 99

Lemon 40, 134, 162, 192

M

Mac & cheese 100

Macadamia nuts 181, 199

Macatias 39

Mango 146, 199, 213

Matcha 218

Mayonnaise 78, 106

Mie goreng 124

Miso caramel 43

Mochi 218

Mole sauce 152

Muffins 162

Mushrooms 58, 60, 70, 77, 99, 127, 156

N

Naan 73

Nachos 141

O

Oats, rolled 199

Olives 67, 68, 84, 90, 134, 138

Onions 121, 138

P

Pain perdu 53

Palak paneer 112

Pancakes 43, 155

Parmesan, non-dairy 102

Passion fruit 199

Pasta 100, 102

Pastry 172, 192

Pasty dough 148

Peaches 95

Peanut butter 62, 77, 78, 122, 142, 165, 190

Peanut sauce 122, 213

Peanuts 146

Pecan nuts 172, 215

Peppers 68, 93, 137, 148, 152

Pepper cream 137

Pesto 68, 83, 133

Petit pois 106

Pickles 83

Pico de gallo 141

Pilaf 115

Pineapple 118, 133

Pissaladière 138

Pistachios 40, 96, 168, 194

Pita bread 80

Pizza dough 138

Polenta 106

Popcorn 207

Porridge 50, 58

Potatoes 100, 130, 137

Pralines 202

Pretzels 161

Prunes 172

Pumpkin 73, 84

Q

Quiche lorraine 110

Quinoa 84, 93

R

Radishes 130

Raspberries 40, 155, 168, 200

Ratatouille 93

Red lentils 80, 116

Rice 115, 116, 121, 194

Rice bacon 70

Rice bars 199

Rice crackers 118

Rice noodles 124, 127

Rice pudding 194, 220

Rice, sticky rolls 213

Risotto 99

Rocket 83, 133

Roll, cinnamon 36

Rougail 142

S

Salad 90, 95, 105, 116

Samosas 146

Satay sauce 77

Sesame seeds 162, 218

Shortbread 190

Smoothie bowl, chocolate 44

Smoothie bowl, sweet potato 47

Socca 90

Soy protein 121

Spinach 58, 60, 84, 112

Sponge cake 207, 216

Sticky toffee puddings 215

Strawberries 167

Sweet potato 47, 54, 118, 146, 148

Sweetcorn 58, 124, 148

T

Tacos 152

Tahini 90, 96, 105

Tahini sauce 184

Tahini, black 162

Tapenade 134

Tempeh 122, 124

Tiramisu 216

Toast 54, 62

Toffee sauce 215

Tofu 68, 110, 172, 196, 210, 216

Tomato caviar 134

Tomatoes 58, 67, 87, 93, 95, 112, 121, 142, 152

Tortilla 137

Tortilla chips 141

Trifle 207

V

Vanilla cream 210

Vegetable patties 60

Vinaigrette 95, 99

W

Walnuts 133

White beans 58, 87, 90, 141

Y

Yogurt 96, 105, 106, 137, 141, 151, 184, 196, 216

Yogurt sauce 80, 90, 151

ACKNOWLEDGEMENTS

Thank you to everyone I've been lucky enough to meet on my journey who, with their advice and support have contributed in one way or another to bring my projects to life.

Thank you to my mother for instilling in me at an early age the importance of a healthy, varied and balanced diet to nourish my body and soul.

Thank you to my father for making me aware of the beauty of nature, and for always supporting me in my appetite to discover the world, even letting me go to the Galapagos Islands when I was 12.

Thank you to my older sister for being the caring and inspiring person she has always been, and for showing me that everyone is free to make their own choices and is the sole master of their own life.

Thank you to Marie Laforêt for trusting me from the very first moment to create this book, and for advising and guiding me throughout this project.

Thank you to Diane and Didier from Solar Editions for their boundless commitment and understanding at every stage on the path to create this book.

Thank you to all of you who follow me on my adventures and who give me the desire and energy to pursue my dreams with the zeal to go further and further! You are my greatest driving force.

Thank you to everyone who follows and supports me from all around the world. You are the proof that the love for good food has no borders and will continue to bring humans together.

And finally, thank you to Clément, my travel companion, my assistant photographer, my official taster, my advisor, my greatest daily support, without whom none of this would exist.

Published in 2023 by
Grub Street
4 Rainham Close
London
SW11 6SS

Email: food@grubstreet.co.uk
Website: www.grubstreet.co.uk
Twitter: @grub_street
Facebook: Grub Street Publishing
Instagram: grubstreetpublishinguk

Copyright this English language edition
© Grub Street 2023

ISBN: 978-1-911667-92-6
A CIP catalogue for this book is available from the British Library.

Published originally in French as *Vegan World*
© 2022 Éditions Solar, a division of Édi8, Paris
All photographs in this book are by Alice Pagès.
Graphic design and illustrations: Cherry Heurteur

Printed and bound by Finidr, Czech Republic